Only the

Wild Goose

Knows

ONLY THE WILD GOOSE KNOWS

ISBN: 978-1-944962-39-5 (paperback)
Library of Congress Control Number: 2017939974

Secant Publishing, LLC
P.O. Box 79
Salisbury, MD 21803

www.secantpublishing.com

Only the
Wild Goose
Knows

SUSAN YARUTA-YOUNG

SECANT
PUBLISHING

To a wonderful traveling storyteller, Beth Vaughan,
who was known to many listeners of all ages, once
upon a time, as "Biddy O'Byrne";
Eastern Shore writer Mary Wood; and
Frank vanLatum, a dear Dutch pal,
who has lived and worked in France
since he was eighteen

Prologue

After crossing the east span of the Chesapeake Bay Bridge, continue traveling on Route 301 for fifteen miles, then turn left onto Route 213 and follow signs for Chestertown. On this quieter, two-lane country road, you'll pass mile-long, tree-lined private driveways. If you slow and look down these drives, you may see houses built during the 1700s and 1800s. Once upon a time, this land was a colony of England. After 1776 many of these estates became American plantations. Here in Queen Anne's County, men and women struggled with an important decision: support the Union or the Confederacy during the War Between the States, also known as the Civil War.

On November 10, 1984, Fred drove with Max and Charles up Route 213. They passed little villages surrounded by rolling fields where farmers had recently harvested corn, soybeans, pumpkins, and squash. They saw miles of bright white-painted fences, padlocked pastures where racehorses grazed. A few mares, stallions, and geldings lifted their heads, looked at the little red truck and snorted. Some began running. Breezes filled manes and tails like sweeping brush strokes on Japanese paintings, trots became rocking canters, faster turning into gallops, heads high into the sky. No longer were they bay quarter horses, golden palominos, dappled gray Arabians, but instead, if you used your imagination (as Max did), they became part of the landscape. Now they were wind-blown free grasses waving in fields, leaping, flying like milkweed until . . . they disappeared. Had they turned into clouds? Would they become horses again at dusk when locked in fresh, straw-filled stalls, noses nudging deep into buckets, lips smacking as they fed on molasses grain? And, after a night's rest when they were out again, where the sky was filled with vees of geese and the noise of their leader's honking commands, air all a-crinkle with the fragrance of drying leaves, reeds, and grasses . . . would the horses again morph away from fur bodies and become one with their surroundings? What images to puzzle on when venturing into the unknown.

After the town of Centreville, Fred took another left. This public road narrowed until it was tunneling through a forest mix of November's nearly bare hardwood trees and always green, bushy, long-needled white pines, tall cedars, and firs straight with dark, bristling boughs. Blue spruce were chubby, hunched trees which seemed to waddle in their planted places. The taller pines were harvested for telephone poles, but once upon a time they'd been masts for schooners. Even now, some sailors preferred these tall, straight trunks for sailboat masts.

Was it odd there were no other cars on the road that day? Or were Fred, Max, and Charles traveling when others were away or resting in their cozy homes? But there they were, alone: no cars ahead, no cars behind.

The road was straight with an occasional half-moon curve. It rolled up and down, though no one from lands of mountains and valleys would have described it as hilly. Instead the land rolled, like pie dough spread on a floured surface before a baker's rolling pin begins flattening it. Like some dough, this road had lumps, smooth spots, and scalloped edges.

Then, after riding for what seemed too long, the boys saw the road ahead became a "Y." Would they continue on the main road or take a smaller lane off to the right? The boys wondered what Fred would do.

Fred went right. For a moment Max and Charles believed they were still traveling on a public road, until they looked ahead and saw two gray cedar posts and a sheep-wire fence sagging under the weight of weed and age.

On both sides, on the right and on the left, ancient trees formed two crooked lines, their battered trunks scarred from years of being pruned back. Entering this old-tree world, Max was reminded of gnomes with hidden eyes, standing as tall as their roots would allow them. Left and right, the trees reached towards each other, limbs forming an arch over this path and their twigs like interwoven, twisted fingers.

The lane was rough and rutted, reducing a driver's speed to no faster than a walking pace. Max felt as if he was entering someplace different from any park, farm, or wilderness adventure he'd ever experienced before.

For a few moments he felt like he was falling asleep, not entering an earthly place at all, but a dream. A dream he'd dreamed before, once or twice or more, and had always hated when it ended. But this was no dream, and they all were entering a new place awake, wondering, not knowing, but feeling as if something special, wonderful, maybe even mysterious, was about to begin.

The truck slowed. Stopped. Fred switched the engine off.

"We're here!" he said.

Charles was waiting for Max, and Max couldn't move. Not yet. Max just wanted to continue looking because, he thought, *'Perhaps . . . if I get out of the truck, what I'm feeling will disappear.'*

Moments, which seemed to Charles like hours, passed.

Reluctantly, Max slid out of the truck's cab. But instead of feeling like the wonder had ended, he realized they'd stepped into a new beginning.

Chapter 1

Early Saturday Morning,
Veterans Day Weekend 1984

7: 45 a.m. outside the house. Fred stood beside the open tailgate to his 1984 Labor Day Weekend Sale Special: a brand-new, extended cab, fire-engine red pickup truck. In the morning sunlight its new wax job made it sparkle like stars across a clear night sky. In Fred's left hand he held a clipboard with yellow paper pad attached, in his right hand his pen. It was countdown time and he was ready with his "Make Sure We Have Everything" list.

Beside him, Mom struggled to hold snowsuit-bundled, seven-month-old, wiggling, gurgling, smiling, clutching-at-everything baby Carrie. As for older brother Ralph, he was sleeping in. Mom would wake him at 10 a.m. At 11 he was due to meet his study partner and FOREVER (as Charles would say) girlfriend, Turkey Legs Toni, to study for mid-semester exams in physics, math, and literature.

"Backpacks packed for an overnight?" Fred asked.

"Including change of underwear, two pairs of socks, extra pants, dress clothes, toothbrush, toothpaste, and deodorant?" Mom asked.

"Yes!" Charles and Max said in unison.

"Boots, hats, and winter coats?" Mom asked.

"Yes, Mom," they groaned.

"Sleeping bags and pillows?" Fred added.

Charles looked at Max. Max looked at Charles.

"Did you?" they asked each other.

Fred laughed. "Not to worry. Your mom has packed them already."

Mom nodded. She dodged Carrie's fingers attempting to pluck her bottom lip.

"Snacks to munch until we stop for brunch/lunch?" Fred asked.

"Right here," said Mom, pointing her boot toe to an extra big, brown paper bag beside her. "Be sure not to mess up Fred's clean cab with cookie crumbs, grape seeds, or apple skins. You'll find a travel package of baby wipes, napkins, and a plastic trash bag for the mess. Your camp bottles are filled with fresh cold water from the spring. That way, if you dribble or spill, you won't leave drips on the seats."

Charles and Max understood. Their mom was an experienced mother who was used to the "Oops! Sorry!" scenes which happened almost daily riding in her van.

"I've almost reached the end of my list. Homework you might have? Books to read? Extra notebook paper and pens for writing?" Fred asked.

"Yes, sir," Max and Charles said.

"I finished my homework last night," Charles added.

Max sighed. "I have a couple of pages left. I promise, I'll get them done."

"Lastly," Mom said, handing baby Carrie over to Fred. "Hugs all around. Have a wonderful time."

They took turns hugging Mom and sneaking loving squeezes on Carrie's little hands, arms, and legs. For a baby sister, Max, Charles, and even Ralph voted Carrie a cool addition to the family.

"Bathroooooooooooooooooooooom!" Fred said in his booming voice. He checked his watch. "Three minutes until takeoff."

At exactly 8, they were all in the truck. In the truck's bed, protected under the cap cover and inside a medium-sized travel cage, Miss Starry Eyes nestled down for the ride. She was a Canada goose their Grandma had raised, a gosling orphan when found three years before.

Chapter 2

A Place They'd Never Been Before

They were a mile from home when Charles asked Fred, "So, where did you say we're going? What will we be doing? And why do we have Starry Eyes with us?"

"Gee, Charles, I thought you'd never ask," Fred said with a grin.

"Well, I was, ah, waiting for you to tell us. I mean, I don't want to spoil some surprise you have planned, but if there's something you can tell us . . . Well, it sure would be cool to know."

His mom once said Charles was eight years old going on forty, meaning he was someone who liked to be organized, planned ahead, and disliked surprises.

Max, who was eleven, was the opposite. He loved to explore, had an active imagination, secretly wrote stories and even poems. He loved to read, but when he was exploring outside he left books behind, with the exception of field guides. He always took notepads, paper, pencils and pens, just in case he might want to make sketches, write notes, jot down names, dates, interesting quotes, and lists of things he'd seen. Sometimes these written sketches became poems or ideas for essays and stories.

"We're taking a trip into a part of the Eastern Shore where you've never been before. We've not going to travel as far as we did when we went to the 'End of the World,' Elliott Island. In fact, we should be at our destination in two hours or so, factoring in traffic jams or the time it takes for our most important stop: lunch," Fred said.

"And the destination of this trip is?"

"Well, Charles," Fred said. "Once we arrive at Mary's home, the longest part of the car trip will have ended. But the adventure of exploring new places, meeting people from other countries or who have traveled to places you and I have only read about, seen pictures or specials on TV . . . will only have begun."

"OK, that sounds pretty cool. Any more details?"

"Hey, Charles, why don't you just relax and let it all happen?" Max suggested.

"Is that what you're going to do?" Charles asked Max.

"Yes, I am."

"OK, but if I begin flying off like some skinny, no-weight guy holding onto a bunch of helium balloons, will you make sure I don't drift away into some twilight zone?"

"YES! Of course!" Fred and Max said at the same time. They laughed.

Chapter 3

Max's Memory of Ocean City

Crossing the bridge, Max looked down at the Chesapeake Bay. The waters were choppy with white crests. Seeing the Bay all gray with white suds, he remembered a Thanksgiving vacation, five years ago, in the old days when their mom was a single mom. A time before she met Fred.

Thanksgiving Day 1979. Ralph, Max, Charles, and Mom went to Grandma and Grandpa's. The traditional feast was cooked and baked from recipes Grandma had learned from her mom, who had learned from her mom and back many generations of moms. German and Irish recipes, not written down but remembered: turkey stuffed with chestnut dressing, hot sweet-and-sour purple cabbage, sauerkraut with pickled pork, giblet gravy. And for dessert there were pumpkin pie and Great-Grandma's German apple cake made from apples Max and Charles had gathered from the orchard by the pond. There was also a favorite family dish that Mom always made: sweet potato casserole topped with toasted marshmallows. Later in the day, the dessert with leftover snacks was Grandma's homemade meringues, baked tan and crispy, served with vanilla ice cream and fresh sprigs of peppermint raised year-round in Grandpa's hothouse.

Early the next morning, Ralph stayed home to study schoolwork and hang out with Grandma, Grandpa, and friends from school. But Max, Charles, and Mom had gone on vacation to Ocean City, Maryland. The van was filled with suitcases, beach toys, and a cooler stocked with Thanksgiving leftovers.

"Oh, the 'Bird Place'. Can't wait!" Max cheered when Mom told him where they were going to stay.

Mom had taken the boys there ever since Charles was a year old, the year their father had said goodbye to them and moved far, far away to begin a new life, in a new house with someone else. Occasionally he'd send a note, toy, or card if he remembered. He'd never been home much before Charles was born. Max's earliest memories were of his parents talking very loud at each other and Mom crying afterwards.

'No sad thoughts,' Max said to himself. Instead, good memories about being small with Mom and Charles on a Thanksgiving vacation long ago.

At the Bird Place, Mom always got a third-floor suite with a kitchen, two bedrooms, one bath, a large living room and a balcony facing the ocean. Down the steps on the bottom floor was an indoor tropical jungle: palm trees, huge plants, two swimming pools. It was a miniature world with ponds, streams filled with large orange goldfish, and arched wooden bridges to cross. In this warm, glassed-in world there were cockatoos and talking parrots, large toy animals to bounce or rock on, a loft full of books, puzzles, board games and building blocks, even a café serving fancy fruit drinks made especially for children and decorated with cherries, oranges, and tiny umbrellas.

There were family saunas, hot tubs, one big swimming pool and a small one, both with lifeguards watching. It was always warm, fun, safe, with other children to play with. AND right outside there was the ocean.

Some years it was cold. They would bundle up in snowsuits and boots when walking where the beach was beaten hard by crashing waves. Or they would sit in sheltered dune spots, protected from the wind, where the sand seemed as high as mountains and soft as powder.

Then there had been years when it was almost as warm as summer. They would take their red, yellow, and blue toy shovels, two green plastic buckets and, with Mom's help, build sandcastles. When the towers were done, they decorated them with shells they'd collected on walks down the beach. They always dug shallow moats.

"Your castles are so lovely that ocean queens and kings will take them as gifts for their royal daughters and sons," Mom always told them.

The year Max was five and Charles was three had been a warm year. During the daytime they didn't even need sweatshirts; instead of snow boots they wore flip-flops. They walked and ran, racing down to the waves and back, as the foamy surf came sliding up, up, closer, closer, chasing them. It had been a day for building three castles, one each, all as gifts to the ocean princesses and princes.

Later, after a conversation with their favorite parrot, Pete, after a swim, and after sitting with Mom in the giant hot tub, it was time for carryout Chinese and leftover apple cake. They sat at the little dining table near the balcony. The sliding glass door was open a few inches so they could hear and smell the ocean while they ate.

Just before sunset, Max went out on the balcony while Mom was busy with Charles. The clouds had gotten thicker. In some places they were dark gray. Up high he saw islands of blue sky, and there were places where the sun on the clouds made them glow sparkling white.

"Mom, come and bring Charles. Come see the sky," Max called.

Mom scooped up Charles, wrapping him in his red Snoopy sleeping bag, and carried him out to join Max. She sat with Charles on her lap. Max was wrapped in his own blue-and-yellow Cookie Monster sleeping bag. He had his own chair.

The glowing white clouds became slim and slimmer as slices of color hedged through them.

Max remembered that he had yelled to Mom: "Pink!"

He remembered how Charles yelled: "Cotton candy! Cotton candy!"

Their mom whispered: "Darker than pink. I think maroon."

The wind blew harder. Seagulls spread their wings and soared on the gusts. Then Max looked down at the ocean. Waves were rolling up, up, up, breaking white like snow, like an avalanche he'd watched on a TV show with Grandpa. Great avalanche waves and suds rumbling onto the hard-packed *sand. He knew all the castles they'd made were now with the sea's royal children.*

Then he saw something: "Mom! Mom! Look!"

There were dolphins arching over and through the giant waves. Great, gray, half-moon shaped backs with moonlight-like white undersides. Four, five, six great creatures bounding over the rolling waves. They were traveling north, passing right in front of their balcony.

"A special sunset, Charles. A special nature moment, Max," Mom said. "Make a wish. Make a good one! I will, too."

Max always remembered the dolphins, the sunset, and the wish he'd made. A few times, when he'd begin to forget it, he'd look at the painting Mom made of that very special nature moment. And when his wish came true, the memory of that moment only grew.

Now, Mom was happy and married to a great guy named Fred. Max had gotten his wish: to have a dad, someone who liked kids and kids liked him back. And it had happened.

Chapter 4

The Chesapeake Bay Bridge and Ferry Boat Stories

Now, on this Saturday in 1984, Max remembered how the ocean had looked five years ago. Now, Mom was home having quiet time with baby Carrie, and Ralph was studying hard for his senior-year SATs. Charles was eight and definitely not a toddler anymore.

Max looked down at the Chesapeake Bay. He saw rough waves rolling as gray as the backs of those dolphins he'd seen and whitecaps like their bellies. The wind was gusty. He felt it smacking against the red truck. He looked at Fred's face, then at his hands gripping the steering wheel so firmly his knuckles were white. Fred was creeping at 25 mph, obeying the blinking yellow speed warning sign.

"Scary. Lots of wind, huh, Fred?" Max said.

"Yep, but it'll be OK. Be brave. Look! We're almost

on the Eastern Shore. See the marsh and how the waves are making those reeds sway? OK, we're on land again."

"Yay!"

"Did you know," Fred said, breathing normally again after the tense crossing, ". . . did you know the Chesapeake Bay Bridge is considered one of the scariest bridges . . . in all the world?"

"What?" Max asked.

"No, really?" Charles questioned.

"Yes. It is. Do you guys know when the Bay Bridge was built?"

"Hmm, I just saw it when we drove on . . . 1952?" Charles asked.

"Bingo!" said Fred. "Yep, that was when it first opened. But long before that, believe it or not, in the 1880s, people started talking about building a bridge across the Chesapeake Bay."

"Like a hundred years ago?" Max asked.

"Yep, like a hundred years ago. They figured if they had a bridge then they wouldn't worry as much when stormy weather brought crashing waves. Long ago, busy ferry boats were used regularly, crossing back and forth connecting the Western Shore to the Eastern Shore."

"In 1907 people stopped gossiping, arguing, debating about building a bridge and actually decided to do it," Fred said. "The decision was made. They were going to build a bridge from Baltimore to Tolchester Beach, a very popular resort to visit back then."

"Let me guess. They built it and it sank?" Charles quizzed.

"Nope. They had plans for the construction and everything, but that all got scratched in 1929."

"Uh oh, I know what happened that year," Max said. He raised his hand as if in school.

Charles looked at Max and his raised hand.

Max quickly dropped his hand. He blurted out, "In 1929 the stock market crashed."

"Exactly," said Fred. "And then came. . .?"

"The Great Depression, followed by World War II," Max said. He smiled at Fred, then Charles. "We just finished studying it in school this week right before vacation. I took the test on Thursday. Think I passed?"

"If those were the questions on it, I vote yes," Fred said. "But after World War II, they finally built it, and the Chesapeake Bay Bridge opened on July 30, 1952."

"You said it's called one of the scariest bridges in the world," Charles said. "Why's that?"

"A memory like an elephant, Charles. You brought us back to my original history lesson," Fred laughed. "There are four reasons: too narrow, no shoulders, low guard rails, and dangerous in high winds, like today. Sometimes they close it down when the winds are too high. And I can tell you, all of those reasons do make it a scary bridge to drive on."

"Yeah, I saw your hands. Man, you were really holding on," Max said. "White knuckles and everything. I was getting scared just watching."

"But we made it."

"Going back home, hopefully we'll have better weather, but then again, we'll be on the westbound bridge. What's its story?" Charles asked.

"Well, it opened in 1973. As you know, it has three lanes, guard rails, and is not quite as scary. At the time when it was designed, people thought the two bridges would be all that would ever be needed and there'd never be any backups, but . . ."

"Big backups happen all the time," Charles said.

"How long are the bridges?" Max asked. "It feels like forever to cross."

"Great question. The bridges are 4.3 miles long. When the eastbound bridge was built, it was one of the longest bridges in the world," Fred said.

"The Chesapeake Bay divides Maryland, right?" Charles asked.

"Yes, but people found ways across. George Washington took the ferries across many times back before the war. Meaning, of course, the American Revolution," Fred said.

"Grandma told us she took ferries all the time when she was going to college in Baltimore and her family lived on the Eastern Shore," Max said.

"Yes, she told me the ferry ride took 40 minutes on a good day. But if the weather was bad, the ferry waited until the weather calmed down and Bay waters were not too rough. Travelers faced delays. When Grandma was going to Baltimore, on good weather days, ferry riders could walk on, but many took cars. Everybody lined up and waited. When the ferry was ready, there was a loud steam blast. After all the cars were parked, drivers and passengers would climb upstairs to an enclosed deck for something hot or cold to drink. As they crossed the Bay, they could socialize with others."

"Ferries ran all night long, right?" Charles asked.

"No. Actually, they didn't. The first ferry would leave at 5 a.m. Back and forth across the Bay, from east-to-west and west-to-east. The last ferry of the day left at 2 p.m. You had to get up early. And you had to be fast, if you wanted to get to an evening destination, otherwise you'd spend the night on a shore you had planned on leaving that day," Fred said.

"Like avoiding rush-hour backups on expressways back home," Max said.

"Yep," said Fred. "The ferry captains were Eastern Shore folk who worked on the water all of their lives. They knew the Bay like they knew . . . well, like the back of their hands. I read that a ferryman once said he could 'smell his way across the Bay' and drive the ferry right into its slip even when it was snowing a blizzard, sleeting ice, or during downpours."

"That's impressive. I'd never want a job *that* scary and hard," Charles said.

"Right. OK, let's connect some crazy dots in this story," Fred said. "Remember when I mentioned Washington State and Seattle?"

"Uh huh," both boys said.

"When Maryland no longer needed ferries to cross the Chesapeake Bay, they sent them to places where they'd be useful. And one place that uses ferries all the time is Seattle. Two Maryland ferries were sold to Washington State: the Gov. Herbert R. O'Conor, which was rechristened Rhododendron, or Rhody, after the state flower, and the Gov. Harry W. Nice, renamed the Olympic. I'd say that's a great example of recycling, wouldn't you?"

"Cool! Named for Olympic National Park in Washington State?" Max asked.

"True, and the Olympic Peninsula," Fred said.

"Guess I'm ready to write a paper for extra credit: 'Some History of the Chesapeake Bay'," said Max. He turned and looked out the window. He was searching for some of his favorite buildings, road signs, and nature spots along Route 50. He searched but saw none. That's when he realized things looked very different. *'Where were they? What was going on?'* he thought. He opened his mouth and said . . .

Chapter 5

"Guess We're Not on Route 50 Anymore"

"Hey Fred," Max said. "Things don't look familiar to me. Are we still on Route 50?"

"Nope," said Fred. "We're on Route 213. This is the road we'll take on our journey back in time through villages and fields which once were plantations. Some are still farms. This road leads us to Centreville, Church Hill, and Chestertown. It's the way to our destination . . . to a place . . . well, a place that looks like time forgot it, but it's written about in the history of America."

"Farming history . . . ah, I'd rather take a nap," Charles said, faking a yawn.

"Well, I won't mind if you nap, but don't fall asleep believing this is the land of nod."

"Huh?"

"Yes, it is farmland, but this farmland was where

people suffered when harvest yields were low, when shipping waters were blocked by battles, when land was fought over by other countries. Here, right here, where fields seem quiet and safe, early American colonists braved arrows zinged from the bows of native tribes. Then came musket blasts from trained European soldiers fighting to reclaim land they believed was stolen by the Maryland Militia: wild and unruly, freedom-seeking colonists."

"OK, forget the nap," Charles said.

"These white-fenced fields where racehorses are grazing?" Max asked.

"Yes," Fred said. "Much of this land was once upon a time large plantations covering miles. Owners divided their land into peach orchards, corn-or grain-fields before it sloped down to become sandy shores lapped by the Chester River. The Chester was an important waterway leading into the Chesapeake Bay. Ships traveled on it to port cities like Baltimore, north to Philadelphia, New York, Boston, and Castine, which is in Maine, and all the way up into Canada. Other cargo was southbound as far as Havana, Cuba. Goods were loaded and unloaded at large docks in Centreville and Chestertown. Then, turn the pages of history books a few chapters closer to our time and what happened? We read about the years when plantations and little towns in Talbot, Dorchester, Kent, and Queen Anne's counties saw their sons heading north to join with the Union Army. Sometimes, in the same family, another brother fled to Virginia to train and join the Confederate Army.

Some of the men trained down south came home and joined the newly formed First Maryland Cavalry of the Confederate Army."

"Fred, you're saying down here one farm might be for the Union and across the field a neighbor might be Confederate?" Max asked.

"Yes. In this same county, one church would support the Union, while nearby another church supported the South. The division showed up in rival small-town papers. Newspapers were a big thing back then. For instance, later today, we're going to Chestertown, where two papers clashed: the *Kent News* (now called the *Kent County News*), which favored staying with the Union, and the *Conservator*, which supported the South. The *Conservator* was shut down and its publisher found himself behind bars in Baltimore for a short time. Later, he was sent to work down in Richmond, Virginia. There were newspapers in support of the Confederates printed in Cambridge, Easton, and even in another town we'll be visiting, Centreville. The division was not limited to those training to become soldiers, or journalists with sharpened quill pens. There's this legendary story of a group of ladies, who lived close to Easton. These ladies made Union soldiers angry by refusing to honor the American flag," Fred said.

"So, ah . . . I mean this is Veterans Day weekend and you're telling us these war stories of long ago because . . ." Max began.

". . . You must have a reason, right?" Charles finished. Fred gave his schoolteacher's smile. "I think I'm not going to say another thing from a history textbook and allow you to figure out the answers to your questions as the day goes on."

Before the boys could think what to say next, Fred slowed the truck to a crawl, tapped his turn signal on, made a right, and soon they were parked in front of a little white with pink-and-purple trimmed house with a sign on its roof:

Chapter 6

Miss Bee's Breakfast Boost Where Chestertown's Hungry Come to Chow Down and Roost

"Time for breakfast/brunch," Fred said.

The boys looked at each other. They didn't say a word, but both wondered why Fred had picked *this* place as *the* place to stop for brunch. Finally, after Fred had locked the truck and before they went in, Max nerved up to ask, "Ah, Fred, you've been to this place . . . this Miss Bee's, before?"

"Oh, yeah. I've 'roosted' here plenty of times. Relax guys. Trust me, Miss Bee's is 'the spot' in all of Chestertown for a fill-up. Come on."

Fred led them to a worn and grubby front door. Near the door, on the ground, someone had placed a crock bowl filled with fresh water. Nailed to the restaurant's outside wall was a gray-and-pink metal box with the words "Free Treats" painted in purple and cartoon drawings of happy dogs and cats with pet treats shaped like bones and fish.

"Miss Bee offers free goodies to the four-legged pets of her customers," Fred explained.

"But not feathered fowl like Miss Starry Eyes?" Charles said.

"Oh, I bet she has something like a bit of leftover crust or pancake." Fred opened the door. "After you, gentlemen."

With the scuffle of tennis shoes, Max and Charles, in that order, slunked in.

They were immediately surrounded by sounds and smells that reminded them of Grandma's kitchen. Cinnamon rolls steamed on counter trays while bacon, ham, and sausages sizzled in frying pans. The roasted fragrance of fresh-brewed coffee blended with the aromas of sweet spicy teas and rich hot cocoa warming the room assured them this was a cozy spot to eat.

"Mmmm," Max and Charles sighed. Maybe Fred was wise in the ways of Chestertown dining spots after all. They stepped aside and waited for him to enter.

As soon as Fred crossed the threshold, closed the door and turned to face the large, open-space dining room, he was warmly greeted by an older woman wearing a purple with pink-dotted dress, and a pink with purple-dotted apron. Her dark round eyes were framed by oversized lavender glasses. Above those colorful rims, the front strands of her snow-white hair were streaked pink. She was shorter than Max, round as soft sofa cushions, but not fat. Someone who liked to fault others might have criticized her. If they used 1980s slang, they might have called her clothes "cheesy", might have labeled her a "ditz", and perhaps chided her energy as "spazzing". Others might have cheered her spirit by calling her "awesome" and "stylish", pointing out her wide-laced, neon pink running shoes.

"Hello, Miss Bee," Fred said.

"Is that you, Freddy? Why, bless my soul! And these must be the two young gentlemen, part of the joyful package deal when you married one of our favorite visiting poets. Welcome! Welcome! Let me scrub down the 'Like-Family' table I hold for dear friends," Miss Bee said.

She snapped up a washcloth and began swiping the pink Formica tabletop. She rubbed away stickiness from its chrome frame. She gave a "lick and a promise" wipe down to the set of chairs, all of which had padded seats upholstered in matching purple vinyl and attached to sturdy metal legs.

"Very 1950s retro," Fred whispered to the boys.

"Is that what it is?" Charles asked.

Both boys looked around the room. There was much to see: framed 1950s menus hung on the walls beside oversize posters advertising "Coca-Cola for 5 Cents," "You Like It, It Likes You. Drink 7 Up!" and "Dad's Root Beer Float Is The Most."

"Imagine Ralph and Toni dressed like this. But this was the style if you were going to the hop!" Fred said, pointing to a drawing of a girl wearing a rose-colored cardigan sweater, black skirt with pink poodle near its hem, saddle shoes, and white bobby socks. Her date was fashionably dressed in a white T-shirt with sleeves rolled (tough-guy style), cuffed blue jeans, and, on his feet, penny loafers. "Since he's dancing fast and furious, my guess is he left his leather jacket back on a hook. Later, they probably sat sipping a soda-fountain milkshake."

"Dressed like Fonzie on *Happy Days*. Geez, Fred, was that how you used to dress when you were a teen? Did you go to hops?" Charles asked.

"Nope. Hops were years before my time. I'm just an old hippie, can't you tell?"

"Oh yeah, well, that works," Max said with a grin. "So is Mom."

Near the table and chairs Miss Bee was scrubbing clean, a lanky young man with bright blue eyes and a mop of blond hair overheard Fred and the boys. He looked up from the egg sandwich he was eating. Immediately, he stood and waved to them.

Recognizing him, Fred smiled and waved back. "Hey, you beat us here!"

Miss Bee looked at them and laughed. "I should have known he was someone you knew, Fred. OK, table and chairs are ready and waiting. I'll be back in a flash with your menus. Today's specials are on the chalkboard under the clock, stage left."

Fred led the boys to the table.

In a light, airy voice with a thick accent, the young man said, "*Bonjour!* I'm Jean!"

"Also known as John," said Fred.

Jean/John and Fred shook hands.

"Pull up and join us. Max and Charles, may I present

Jean, an artist, actor, teacher, man with many talents who's recently arrived in the U.S."

"I *residee dans* . . . in France, but I was born in Holland. Ee's confusion, yeh?" He put out his hand. "Max?"

"Yes, hi Jean." They shook hands. Max moved to one side, making room for Charles.

"*Et* Charles," Jean said, shaking his hand.

"Hi John."

"Jean, join us. Grab the rest of your breakfast and eat before it gets cold. There's plenty of room for all of us here. Pull up a chair," Fred said. He gestured towards the table Miss Bee had prepared. He motioned to the boys.

Jean grabbed his plate, silverware, napkin, and mug of hot tea and pushed his chair close to Fred with a couple of nimble knee nudges.

"Ee's good timing this, eh? Meeting you here for a meal. Meeting Max et Charles before the event," Jean said. He arranged his place setting so he was sitting next to Fred.

"Shh," Fred whispered. "I've not told them of today's plans."

"Ah, mystery theatre. Very good. Bien!" Jean said. He smiled, then bit into his sandwich. "'Scuse me, but my belly has been growling like a verrry big cat. Like the lion roaring before MGM movies begin."

"Here you go! Menus for all of you. Another menu for you, Jean. Fred, I think it'll take a few meals to fill up this young man. I can see ribs though that corduroy jacket he's swimming in," Miss Bee said, handing out menus. "Now, while you read over what we are offering, anybody interested in some hot cocoa with whipped cream? They come with peppermint sticks for stirring."

All said "yes," including Jean. Actually, he said "*oui*."

When Miss Bee returned with heated-just-right Cocoa Delights, she took their orders. Charles, eyes too big for his stomach, chirped: "Bacon, ham, sausage, and three pancakes." He didn't read "pancakes the size of dinner plates" on the menu. Max ordered a cinnamon roll, a sticky bun, and a side of bacon. (Mom's snack pack had been totally on the healthy side with fruit and oranges). Fred picked his usual Eastern Shore power meal: grits, eggs over easy, a slice of ham, and homemade corn muffins. As always, he planned on finishing what the boys couldn't eat.

Miss Bee looked at the skinny young Dutch man who spoke French. "And?"

"Go ahead, really fill up, I've got the check," Fred told him.

"*Merci*," Jean said. "O-key. How 'bout large *frites* — ah, you call them french fries, eh? With mayonnaise in bowl and uncooked greens." He looked at Fred for help. "How you say it?"

"Salad?"

"*Oui*, yes, thankee," Jean said. "Salad. *Bien!*"

French fries with mayonnaise? Charles and Max gave each other the look.

"This is really good timing. And you found Miss Bee's. Was that easy? How did you get here?" Fred asked Jean.

"I took bus to Chestertown, then I put out my thumb . . . I, how do you say it? Hitch a ride, *n'est-ce pas?* Here."

"You hitchhiked? Scary," Max said.

"Oh, thumb-ride not something people do?" Jean looked surprised.

"Well, down this way, here in Chestertown, it was probably OK. But I wouldn't do it in bigger cities," Fred said.

"Ah, *je suis desole* . . . am sorry. At home all the time we do it, *mais ma maison est* . . . hmmm, ah, in country. . . how you say? Village? Like Chestertown."

"Got it. *Bien*, Jean," Fred said. He turned to the boys, "Jean said he was sorry: '*Je suis desole.*' Then he said '*mais ma maison est*', which means 'but my home is.' Jean, I always enjoy your mix of English and French. Max and Charles, I think both your French and your English will get better the more you listen and talk to Jean."

Jean laughed. "I'm Dutch, see, but I live in France since I was out of school. The French people always look at me with funny looks, like this . . ." Jean tilted his head and made several questioning looks: someone with eyebrows raised and mouth open; a look with his hand rubbing his brow; a look with one hand up at his mouth; a look with head wobbling left to right and right to left.

The boys' uptight "let's give this Jean/John guy a hard time" ended on the spot. They joined Fred laughing at Jean's comic characters.

Jean laughed, too. "You learning French in school? You might be helping me out, not with my English only but with my French."

"They only teach us French once a week," Max said.

"*Moi aussi!*" said Charles.

"*Bien!*" Jean said. "But it will be fun teaching each other how to speak better."

"You'll need a ride to performance site #1?" Fred asked Jean.

"*Oui.*"

"Well, it'll be cramped but we can do it. My new truck has a little seat behind the front bench. It's a short trip from here to the performance site."

Max looked at Charles. Charles looked at Max. Both boys mouthed their favorite quote from *Alice in Wonderland,* "Curiouser and Curiouser". They loved how Lewis Carroll allowed Alice to slip into "bad English," plus it just worked as a great code for them to use.

Miss Bee arrived with king-size trays in each hand. Conversation was put on pause by the bliss of eating a huge brunch. For the next 15 minutes it was all chew and no talk, but no one was counting minutes as an Elvis clock on a wall near their table danced time away.

A pause in eating came when Jean dipped his french fries into a soup bowl of mayonnaise, and though he generously offered samples, there were no takers.

"You sure? Ah, it is how they're served in Amsterdam. And in France. Yum," Jean said.

"We're sure!" Max, Charles, and Fred said in unison.

Jean laughed. "But sometime I will get you to try, then maybe you change your minds. Maybe when you come visit me in Europe, I take you and you will see."

At the end of the meal, Fred, Max, and Charles felt stuffed and wondered if they could move, while Jean rubbed his stomach and said, "Ah, feels just right."

Fred thanked Miss Bee.

"No thank you necessary. It's my pleasure to see empty plates and filled tummies."

"Will we see you later at the Veterans Day event?" Fred asked.

"I'll be there . . . but you may not know it's me," Miss Bee said with a wink.

"Well, if the real you is hidden by the part you play and I can't find you, give me a sign so I can applaud extra loud," Fred said.

"Deal! I'll flash you a peace sign, OK?"

"Deal," Fred said. "Hey guys, what do we say to Miss Bee before we leave?"

Together, Max and Charles said "Thank you!"

"*Merci*," said Jean.

Outside of Miss Bee's, Fred gave Jean the tour of his new truck: under the hood, tires, a look inside at the fancy dials on the dash.

Meanwhile Max and Charles climbed up in the truck bed, under the cap, and wiggled between "must take" things stuffed there. They filled Miss Starry Eyes' dish with fresh water they'd brought in gallon milk jugs. They placed feed and leftovers — pancake bits and corn muffin crumbs — in her dish. They watched as she pecked at the goodies, filled her beak with water until it was dripping, stretched out her neck, head up, and in true goose fashion, bobbed down her snack. They stroked her soft feathers, talking to her in goose lingo. And she responded with soft murmuring, grunting, and an occasional louder-pitched "hink, hrink, hrih."

"She's doing just fine," Charles said.

"Yep, she's in a happy, goosey state of mind," said Max.

They crawled out and emptied the truck's back seat of their stuff. The seat was long and wide, but the space between it and the front seats was extremely tight. How would Jean get in? The truck had only the two front doors in its cab.

"Ready to go?" Fred asked. "OK, Jean first."

The boys and Fred watched. First Jean took off his jacket. He flourished it like a matador's red cape then threw it into the truck's back seat. He pressed his arms tightly against the sides of his body, "I an eel," he announced, and leaning back went into the truck headfirst with his back on the bench seat, squirming side to side, snake-like. Moments later his feet and toes were in the air, and then his whole body was in. His head popped up! "*Voila!*" He was sitting with his back against the truck's side, facing front.

"John's got talent," Charles said.

"Indeed, and more to come," said Fred.

Max applauded, then jumped into the truck.

All in, truck started, Max asked Fred if he could put the radio on. It was set on a local Top Ten hits station. Fred nodded yes. Max pushed the button and . . .

"Ghostbusters!"

They all sang along to the popular song. Fred, Mom, and the boys had seen *Ghostbusters* that summer when it first came out in movie theaters.

"Who can we call when we need a helping hand?"

"How 'bout you guys call ghost nabbers?" asked Jean.

After the song was over, Max lowered the volume.

"Oh, my goodness!" Jean said.

"Timely," said Fred.

"Hey Fred," said Charles, "where are we headed now?"

"To a haunted cemetery," Fred said.

Chapter 7

Map Quest

When you're in Chestertown, you're no longer in Queen Anne's County. You're in Kent County. There's no gate, no toll. Traveling on a main road, you may (or may not) encounter signs welcoming you to this ever-changing old world.

Like Queen Anne's, Kent is filled with colonial, pre-Revolution, and Civil War history. It's where you see large farms that once were plantations. On historical road signs, in libraries, visitor centers, museums, churches, town halls, restaurants, parks, and even cemeteries, you can read about life before and after the Emancipation Proclamation.

It's a place where road maps were often still needed to find places because shops, gas stations, even private homes, were miles apart. And in 1984 there was no GPS or smart phones to guide you.

"Hey Max," Fred said.

"Yes?"

"Here, take this road map. I have it folded to show the Chesapeake Bay and Chester River region. See if you can find Chestertown. Then when you find it, start looking for St. Paul's Kent Episcopal Church or St. Paul's Mill Pond or maybe St. Paul's Churchyard."

Max took the road map from Fred. He and Charles began looking for St. Paul's.

"I see the word Kent," Max said. "It's printed in big letters."

"Yes, it means Kent County. That's good. Chestertown is in Kent County. Those lines indicate the county boundaries."

"Oh, OK. I see something about a pond and I see some roads, but I don't see any names on them."

"Probably too small. But good. Can you find St. Paul's Kent?"

"Ah, oh yeah, here it is," Max said, putting his finger on those words.

"Great," said Fred. He found a safe place to pull the truck off the road. Once the truck was stopped, in park and with flashers on, he took the map from Max to look for himself.

"Good work, guys. We're going in the right direction. Only a mile or so more and we'll be there. Thank heavens for good road maps *and* road map readers."

"How 'bout hardest work of all . . ." Jean said from his place behind Fred and the boys. "How 'bout folding map back the way it was new?"

"True," Fred laughed. "I never passed that test."

"It is a hard one, eh?" Jean said. "Shall I try?"

"No, not yet. I need it folded to show this section. Later, I'll put you to the challenge," Fred said.

Chapter 8

The Haunted Tomb and
Meeting the Teller of Tales

After looking at the map, Fred said, "Sandy Bottom Road is where we'll find St. Paul's Kent Churchyard and the cemetery we're looking for . . . 7579 Sandy Bottom Road."

Four sets of eyes looked through the windows. Almost at the same time they saw the sign: "St. Paul's Kent Churchyard." Cars were parked everywhere. There wasn't an empty space anywhere. Where could Fred park?

"Hmm, I'll let you three off. You can find your way into the churchyard. First you'll see the old church. Be sure to read about it. Afterwards, start looking for a grave north of the oldest gravestones. I imagine there'll be a well-worn path to it. I'll meet you there. If you can't find it, I'll meet you at the huge tree. You'll know the one.

It's over 400 years old, the biggest tree in the area: a swamp chestnut. I recall seeing a bench near it, and there's a plaque with information about it." Fred pulled the truck off the road and stopped.

Max and Charles jumped out. Both turned to face the truck. They were eager to see how Jean would exit. Would he "eel" out as he had "eeled" in?

Soon his sock-covered feet appeared, white ankles, pant legs . . . he was rocking right and left on his back. Then feet were on the ground. Next he was bent over, sitting on the edge of the seat. He plopped his shoes out and without looking at his feet figured out which foot to slip into which shoe, didn't even use his hands. Out of the truck, he reached in and grabbed his jacket, which he quickly pulled on over his lightweight cotton shirt. There was a November chill in the air.

"Ah," he said. He wiggled his body up and down from toes to head, then head to toes, three times. "That feels better. I begin to feel like I . . ." he paused, grinned, and gave his "hahah" laugh. ". . . I begin to feel like I cramped in a box, to be slipped into a grave."

"Creepy, John," Charles said.

"Oh, Jean," said Max.

"OK guys, see you soon," Fred said.

They watched the red truck disappear down the car-cluttered, narrow lane.

"O-key, the adventure begin, eh?" Jean said, rubbing his hands. "Which way we go? I think we each find our own way. When we find the place we need to be, we whistle and then we'll be together again, eh?"

"I can't whistle," said Charles. He looked disgruntled.

"I can't always whistle either," admitted Max.

"*N'est-ce pas?* Well, *tant pis . . . Mais . . . Bien!*" Jean held up his hand, index finger pointing to the sky. "I have just the answer to whistling problem." He reached into a baggy jacket pocket and pulled out three little plastic whistles. They were bright red with yellow bands around their middle and shaped like two-inch-long hot dogs in their buns. "Try these. I think pretty good," Jean said, handing out the whistles.

The three tried their whistles, which made sounds much louder than one would imagine.

"Way cool, John," Charles said.

"Great," agreed Max.

"O-key! Ee's good. Now, next problem, but not so much. We need a code. Charles, you are the youngest guy here. So, I say you make the most noise, eh? When you find the grave, you whistle three long times. Max, you next in age, so you whistle two long times . . ."

"And you'll whistle once," said Charles.

"Once, hey, no way! I whistle as many times as I want because, you see, I may look like a big guy, but inside I'm just a baby. Hey, I kid you. I will whistle like this!" Jean blew his whistle.

"Now, *vite*, we go looking for her."

"Who is her?" Charles asked. No one had said the name of the person they were looking for before.

"Ah, you will know, but if not . . . then look for a grave with Mardi Gras beads, a deck of cards, maybe, pack of cigarettes, and, hmm, maybe even some, what they say, booze? Something some grownups drink. Most likely the Russian kind. Vodka," Jean said.

"No way," Charles said. "Vodka on a grave?"

"Charles, you know how someone in Baltimore leaves a bottle of booze on Edgar Allen Poe's grave on his birthday? I guess it's like that," said Max.

"Oh, yeah," said Charles. "OK."

"Commenceer! Let the adventure begin!" said Jean.

Holding whistles in hands, Max, Charles and Jean walked to the old brick church. On a sign they read: "The original building had been built in 1713." St. Paul's Kent was considered one of the oldest churches on the Eastern Shore of Maryland. After reading the sign together, all three took different routes on paths between tombstones, all in search of a grave which might be oddly decorated.

Max headed straight north. He saw very old gravestones, but soon he found himself surrounded by ones with dates he could read: 1800s and 1900s. Then he noticed a well-worn path. It was leading to a stone many people must have visited as the grass was gone and the ground surrounding the grave was bare.

Moving closer he saw strings of purple, green, and yellow beads, flowers, and miniature bottles of vodka. He'd found it! But whose stone was it? He crept up until the toes of his tennis shoes were touching the edge of the stone. He looked down at the engraved writing: "Tallulah Brockman Bankhead." It sounded familiar, but he wasn't sure where he'd heard it.

Before he could blow two long notes on his whistle,

he heard a voice. A voice talking with a strange accent. Speaking in English, but not the kind of English that people used in Maryland in 1984.

Max wasn't sure if he should hide or run away . . . His heart was pounding. He wondered, *'Can this other person hear my heart? It's beating loud as thunder.'* He heard the person speaking:

"Now, ya see how it happens, don't ya'? An' you do understand what I be sayin'? Me, an old woman an' a comin' from a time long ago . . . An' me one that been travelin' so as, well, don't ye know, to sit me down a spell would do me well. Ye mind if I sit here a spell an' rest me achin' feet? Ah, you be a kind one, ye be."

Then Max saw an older woman coming towards him. She was wearing a long, dark blue skirt and had a black shawl around her shoulders. Her face was turned, she was looking back from where she'd come. He saw her silver gray hair pulled away from her face and fastened in an old-fashioned bun, the kind people called a psyche knot. He knew this because he'd seen pictures of his great-grandmother with her hair done this way, and his grandmother told him the name of this famous hairstyle.

Max saw she was carrying a large wicker basket, her arm looped through its handle. He watched her turn towards him and look up.

When she saw Max, it gave her a start.

They both screamed.

"Ahhhh!"

"Ohhhh! Ye!"

A pause. The older woman put her free hand to her

chest, then smiled and said, "Ah, wee boy, ye did give me a scare, ye did."

"Ah, I'm, I mean . . . are you . . . I . . . are you a . . . a ghost?" Max asked.

"Ghost is it you're wonderin' I be? No, not ghost of even a woman from a world long ago. Quite honestly, not even someone from far away. In fact, I live in Maryland, though not on the Eastern Shore."

As the woman spoke, her "old-fashioned" accent began to disappear, and she sounded more like other older women Max had met.

"I can see you're wondering what I'm all about. Well, I'm an actress and a teller of tales. In a little while I'll go in front of an audience and tell a story. Just now, well, I was rehearsing. I'm Beth. Who are you?" she asked.

Max gave a big sigh. "I'm Max. I guess, actually, I was looking for you, but I didn't know what you'd look like."

"Max? And your mom is a poet, right? You're here with your brother Charles and your stepdad Fred, right?"

"Yes. How did you know?"

"Grownups sometimes make plans and keep them as surprises. Someone else might be with you?"

"Yes. Jean from France. Oh, wait excuse me. I have to let Jean and Charles know I've found the grave. And I've found you." He blew his whistle two times as loud as he could. "Sorry, this was the signal Jean suggested. Now we wait and see if he and Charles heard it."

Max looked at Beth. He had many questions and he couldn't keep silent. "Will you be Beth today when you tell stories? Where will you be telling them? How do you know Mom? And . . ."

"One minute. Let me answer these. If you ask too many questions all at once, my old gray head might forget one or two you started with." Beth sat down on a stone near the grave.

"No, I'll not be Beth when I'm on stage. I'll be Wynda Lutair from a time and country far away. Scotland actually, but many years ago. She'll be speaking in the way you heard, telling the tales inside the hall they made out of what was once the Vestry. It's a special program for children, teens, well, for anyone. It's part of today's celebrations. How do I know your mom? We work together through Maryland arts groups . . . we're good friends. As for Jean. Well, Jean I've yet to meet, but I've heard about him."

"Max!"

"Here comes Jean," said Max. "Right behind him is my brother Charles. Hey Jean, over here! Hey Charles!" Max turned to Beth. "Fred had to park the truck. He's supposed to join us as soon as he can find a parking place."

"Good. Now, Max, it may suit me best to not be Beth but Wynda Lutair, as I need to travel about back in time. Do you know what I be talkin' 'bout? I need to be Wynda Lutair so to be ready for storytellin'."

"Cool. I'll explain what you are doing to the others so you can go back into character," Max said. He gave Beth/Wynda a thumbs up.

Jean and Charles arrived together. Jean in a loping canter, Charles scooting around one gravestone after another, then skidding to a sudden stop like a baseball player who's just beaten a throw. He was red-faced, panting, and when he saw Beth, his eyes and mouth became big circles. "Whoa! Who?"

"*Bonjour*," Jean said. He gave a dramatic bow.

"Good day to yah, kind sir."

"Jean and Charles. It is my great honor to introduce you to Wynda Lutair, a storyteller, a teller of tales. Charles, she knows Mom."

"Good day to ye. An' yes, am a teller of tales. I be right pleased to meet you both here where it is lovely with air fresh an' birds singin'."

"Ee, looky great," Jean said, smiling.

He and Beth/Wynda began talking actor shop talk.

Max took Charles to one side. "Charles, Beth will be performing soon . . . and so now she's in character. She doesn't always talk the way she is now. She's one of the reasons Fred couldn't park the truck close to the churchyard, she's performing nearby in the Vestry."

"Oh, OK, got it," Charles said. "Did you find the grave?"

"Yep. Look, here it is. But I don't know who the person is. The name sounds familiar but . . . oh look. I think I see Fred."

"Yeah, it's Fred. Hey Fred, over here!" Charles yelled so loud it made all, including nearby birds, go silent.

Everyone watched Fred make his way between the gravestones. A few feet from them, he applauded. "Good job, boys. Great job, Jean." When he reached the group, he immediately went to Beth and shook her hand. "So wonderful to meet you at last, I've heard so much about you."

"Ah, good day to yah, Fred, it's been a real pleasure a meetin' up with Max an' now all of you. Methinks it be 'bout time I make me way to the Vestry. People expectin' their teller of tales to come in a timely fashion. I hopes ye be plannin' to watch with the rest."

"Indeed, yes." Fred said. "Yes, please, we'll be coming soon. And I know we'll see you after the show."

"I be goin' then. Good day to yah," Wynda Lutair said. She bowed her head and headed up the path towards the Vestry.

"The show begin in . . . ah . . . um, in an hour, but Beth needs to make arrangements with stage people," Jean explained.

"We'll go soon, too, but we have tickets and reserved seats so we have a little time to explore here. Did you find the grave?" Fred asked, looking at the boys and Jean.

"Max find it . . . but we just here *un* moment ahead of you," Jean said.

"The grave is over here," Max said, leading them.

"Wow, look. It's like you said it would be, with different colored beads, a pack of cigarettes, and even . . ." Charles got down closer to the gravestone to look, ". . . a little bottle of vodka. Whose grave is this anyway?" He stared at the engraved letters and read the name out loud. "Tallulah Bankhead, who was she?"

"Ah, she was quite a lay-dee. She acted on big stages in New York City," Jean said.

"Yes, she was an actress on stage but also movies and TV shows. The movie role she was famous for was Connie Parker, a newspaper columnist in the 1944 dramatic adventure movie *Lifeboat*. It was directed by Alfred Hitchcock," Fred said. "The movie is based on a story by writer John Steinbeck. The plot is about American and British ship survivors. Their ship was sunk by a German sub, and they're grouped together in a lifeboat . . . but then some people begin disappearing. Sometime we'll go to a video store and rent it. It's a good movie that catches some of the tension between countries during World War II."

"Steinbeck's books are ones we have to read in school, right?" Max asked.

"Yep, usually *The Grapes of Wrath* and *Of Mice and Men*. Hard stuff. You'll read them in high school," Fred said. "*The Grapes of Wrath* shows the perils of people living through the Dust Bowl era. *Of Mice and Men* is a powerful story about loneliness, poverty, and how people treat each other. But here we are at Tallulah Bankhead's grave. She was a great actress struggling with . . . well, with bad stuff like cigarettes and alcohol. As you can see by her gravestone, she died young."

"Why is a famous New York actress buried here?" Charles asked.

"Because Tallulah Bankhead's sister lived in Chestertown. It was here this famous actress came to get away from crowds and be with her family," Fred said.

"Ees her grave is haunted?" Jean asked.

"People claim if you come here at midnight and put your ear on the stone, Tallulah will talk to you," Fred said.

"Yikes, scary," Max said.

"Creeeepy," said Charles.

"I wondee if I can git someone to go with me and listen tonight," Jean said. He looked at Fred.

"We'll discuss it later," Fred said.

★★★★★★★

"Wynda Lutair is awesome," Charles said.

"Very cool," said Max.

"I totally agree," said Fred.

"*Oui!*" exclaimed Jean.

"I hope Mom has her come over to the house to visit us. Fred, maybe you and Mom will take us to see another of her shows?" Max asked. "I'd like to talk to her and find out how she makes you feel like you're really in the story she is telling, visiting places with her, and not just listening as a story is told. She makes you become one of the characters in it."

"Oh, you'll be seeing more of Beth, if not Wynda, for sure," Fred said.

"It is for real sure, hey?" Jean said, looking at Fred with a grin. "Hey, I need meet up with Beth an' make arrangements. See, I'm to be at next show an' I ride there with Beth so I can prepare . . . like Beth prepared to be Wynda."

"Will you become a Scotsman?"

"Non, even harder for me . . . I need to be an American . . . I need to practice what I say so I say it American and not the usual way. I have only . . . little words to say. I may even git it right, eh? What do you say?"

Max and Charles looked at each other and said, "*Non*, no way!" they laughed.

Max said, "We're just kidding you, Jean."

"You guys are hard judges . . . whew! I may not look your way when I'm on stage or I may git scared then I will jumble lines."

"Ah, John, you'll do great!" Charles said.

Max and Fred seconded Charles' vote.

Chapter 9

Washington College, Then Queen Anne's County Courthouse

Fred, Max, and Charles left the crowd, and Jean, at St. Paul's Kent Vestry.

"Where are we headed now, Fred?" Charles asked.

"While we're here I want to show you Washington College," Fred said.

"Ugh, more history," Charles groaned.

"Washington College, as in D.C. or our first President?" Max asked.

"As a matter of fact, Max, you get an A. The college is named for President George Washington."

"So?" asked Charles, but now he was interested.

"Washington College, first known as Kent Free School, was founded in 1723. It was the fifth college in America."

"The first was Harvard, right?" asked Max.

"Yes, it was. Harvard, located near Boston, was founded in 1636. Then came William and Mary, in Virginia, 1693; St. John's College, Annapolis, Maryland, 1696; Yale, located in Connecticut, 1701." Fred rattled off names and dates.

"I guess the first colleges are all located in places where people first settled when coming to America?" Max asked. "Studying American history in school this year helps, but today, Fred, you're making history become alive with this trip. Seeing these places is better than watching videos in class and assigned readings from our history books."

"Agreed," Fred said.

"Ah, so how did Kent Free School get to be called Washington College?" Charles asked.

"Good question, Charles. Basically, the college asked General George Washington if he'd mind if the college was named after him. After touring the school and learning more about it, not only did Washington not mind, he gave them 50 guineas, over $9,000 in today's money. He went on to serve on Washington College boards and became very involved. The college is probably one of the reasons why he frequently took ferries over the Chesapeake Bay from 1757 until 1791. Sadly, on December 13, 1799, only 30 months after President Washington retired from office and was finally able to enjoy being a wealthy plantation owner, he took sick with a bad fever. He died the next day at his home . . . ah, either one of you know the name of his home and where it was?"

"Um . . . Mount something, near D.C.?" asked Charles.

"Mount Vernon on the banks of the Potomac River, but I'm not sure exactly where," Max said.

"Good job. Mount Vernon it is. And yes, on the Potomac in Virginia, across from Prince Georges County (or as we call it, PG County) in Maryland."

"Right here in Chestertown, the first President of the United States visited frequently. That's pretty cool," said Max.

"It sure is. Look, here's the college entrance," Fred said. He pulled the truck to the curb. They looked at the college and read a big white sign with its name and date.

"Not a huge college campus," Charles said. "Not like the University of Maryland."

"No, but a college with an especially great program for anyone who likes to write. Every year since 1965 one graduating senior who has proven to be a good writer receives a major award: the Sophie Kerr Prize. It's an honor to receive it, and it also carries a cash award, which helps young writers begin their careers."

Max stared at the college campus' brick walkway, at the old and new brick buildings. Fred's description of the writing program and the Sophie Kerr Prize made something inside of him stir, like butterflies in his stomach. He already really liked everything he'd seen in Chestertown. Now, here was a college campus that wasn't scary big, a historic college, a college that nurtured writers. Max was only eleven, but already he'd thought about what he'd like to do when he grew up.

He'd even started thinking about colleges. *'Wow, this is it . . . I really think this is where I want to go . . . if I could only get in. Well, it means study hard. Good grades. Keep writing. Save my money,'* Max thought.

"OK, just wanted to show you the college. Now we're on our way again," said Fred.

They traveled past big farms from Kent County into Queen Anne's County to the village of Centreville.

Fred handed Max and Charles the folded paper map again. "I need you two to find the Queen Anne's County Courthouse. I think it's located right in town. I'm on Route 213, which I think has a name in Centreville, Commerce Street maybe?"

"OK. Here's a road with 213 written under it," said Charles.

"And here's Centreville," Max said.

"And . . . and here's where 213 is called Commerce Street," said Charles.

"And then. . . ?"

"And then I turn here," Fred said. "Look, there's the sign for the courthouse." He pulled into a "Scenic Parking Area" and switched the truck off. "All out. We'll read the sign before we go into town. Town will probably be busy due to the Veterans Day event."

All three read: "Queen Anne's Court House first opened in 1793. It's the oldest courthouse still in use in Maryland." The sign also stated, "located on Broadway between Liberty Street and Commerce (Route 213)."

"Great, we're almost there," Fred said. "Let's hop back in. I'll have to find a parking place near the courthouse."

"When does the 'event' start?" Charles asked.

"At high noon. It's 11:15 now."

"11:15, whoa! We've already done a lot today," Max said.

"Yep, and still a lot to do," said Fred.

Fred found a parking place not far from the courthouse. He and the boys joined the crowd forming around the courthouse steps. On the left side, they saw the American flag unfurled and swishing in a slight breeze. They saw a podium, two chairs, and on the far right side of the stage, not as big, but still unfurled and flying, a Confederate flag.

At exactly noon a woman—dressed in velvet, lace, silk ribbons and bows as a wealthy woman might have dressed during the Civil War—stepped to the podium. Behind her was another woman, also well-dressed in 1860s costume. She stood behind a chair near the American flag. Next, two men entered the stage area. One wore a blue Union uniform and the other was dressed in Confederate gray. They sat.

The woman at the podium welcomed the audience. She gave a brief history of Centreville during the Civil War era. She told of divisions in communities and even within families.

"Here in Centreville we had a group who called themselves 'Confederates for Centreville,' but I'll let Mrs. Smith tell you about them." She turned her back to the audience. There was a ten-second pause, then she turned to face the audience again, a different person, her body stooped; she spoke with a thick Southern accent.

"Our boys were in a quandary as to what to do. Our farms were losing money, and due to blockades, we were having trouble sailing crops to big Baltimore town where they'd be bought or would be put on larger export ships. My one son, Michael, decided he needed to learn to be a soldier. He took himself to New York and was accepted at West Point. My other son, Gabe, was already studying down South in Virginia. That's where he stayed. I prayed every night my sons wouldn't end up fighting against each other in this awful war."

The woman standing behind the chair lifted her head.

Max and Charles recognized her. It was Beth. Now she was in a Civil War play.

"Many of the men who formed the Centreville Confederates had fought in the War of 1812-1814. They were too old to fight in any more wars, some had bad legs or arms wounded while fighting. But even with aches, pains, and old age, they gathered together, organized, and called themselves a Cavalry. They'd ride their horses as fast as they dared, and faster even than they should. They'd meet in each other's barns and, over bowls of punch—and it was not Methodist punch, but spiked—they'd share war stories and make plans for battles."

The other woman looked up. Max elbowed Charles and whispered, "Miss Bee."

"I know," said Charles. "I was just about to tell you."

They looked at Fred, who looked at them and put his finger in a "shhh" sign.

"Now, those Confederates for Centreville devised a

plan and off they went as a group to Baltimore. Their mission was to buy many weapons and bring them home to make war against Yankees who'd gathered here and there around our Eastern Shore. Because of riots in Baltimore, there were no guns to be had. But our boys didn't return home empty-handed. They did not return with muskets or pistols, like they'd planned; instead, they came home with the most massive load of gunpowder we folks in Centreville could have ever imagined. And do you know what those boys did?"

The young man sitting in the chair nearest her stood. He took off his Confederate cap and his fuzzy blond hair shown in the bright sun. With a grin and sparkling blue eyes he said, in a thick southern accent, "We took all the gunpowder we could scoop and we hid it. Yes, sir, we did. We hid it where no Yankee could of found it. Nor never did."

"Jean?"

"John?"

"Shhh! Yes," said Fred.

The other young man stood up. He took off his Union cap and his long red hair shown in the sun. "We heard rumors the Rebels had done this, but we never knew for sure. We never did find it. We marched back and forth in lines. We even had fine local ladies siding with the Rebels give us dirty looks and even a few, as sweet as you'd think they might be, sweet, dignified, elderly, gentle ladies, come marching right by us and refused to even acknowledge the flag. We were proudly flying our dear Stars and Stripes. We gathered together and sang 'The Anthem': *'Oh say can you see'*. But those ladies looked the other way."

"Some anger. Some fights. But no battlefields here. And as for that gunpowder. Well, wait, let me have these two young men shake hands."

The man dressed in Union uniform and Jean, dressed as a Confederate, came forward and shook hands. They smiled at each other. They even slapped each other on the back.

"And peace, though at times a prickly peace, was restored," Miss Bee and Beth said together.

"If you're still a-wondering about where the gunpowder was stored," Miss Bee said, "well, it was stored right here. A massive load of gunpowder stored right here in the basement of the Queen Anne's County Court House. But you can rest easy, it's long gone now. Or so I've been told."

A group of five people dressed in Civil War period clothes, though not uniforms, came out onto the steps. They each carried a musical instrument: snare drum, flute, two trumpets, and a French horn.

Beth said to the audience, "Now, if you all will please sing with us, we'll join our voices in joyful peacefulness and sing our 'American Anthem'."

The band played a few notes and then, led by the group on the steps of the courthouse, all sang the anthem, also known as "The Star Spangled Banner."

At the end, actors and musicians bowed and the audience applauded.

As he clapped his hands, and while the boys were

close, Fred instructed them on what would happen next. "Now, after we congratulate the actors, it's back to the truck and back to Chestertown. We have a 'tea party' to attend as guests of our hostess. She's the tall woman with short white hair who just hugged the Yankee actor. That's Mary, and the Yankee is her son, Gabe."

Chapter 10

Meeting Mary and the Chestertown Tea Party

There was no re-enactment of the Chestertown Tea Party on November 10, 1984. The reenactment *had* happened, but on Memorial Day Weekend, as it does every year. Maybe in 1985, they would attend it.

At 1 p.m. Fred, Max, and Charles, joined by Jean and Beth, met Gabe and his mother, Mary. They were Mary's special guests at a restaurant on Chestertown's waterfront, near where tea had been thrown in the water on May 23, 1774.

"Well, at last we meet! You must feel like today has been such a wild-goose chase! You poor travelers from the Western Shore. Fred, it has been simply ee-ons since I saw you . . . when you were a free man courting a woman with three children. And here you married my poet friend and you two have added a girl baby to the household of boys. And here you are . . . let me see: tall, older one, must be Max. How do you do? Then a younger, but old in many ways (or so I've heard), Charles. How do to you?" Mary shook hands with each.

"Welcome all of you to my absolutely favorite restaurant here on the water. Prepare yourselves for a feast. Oh, you must remember, it's no longer crab season. We're entering the height of oyster season delights. I hope you like oysters. They are an acquired taste," Mary cautioned, looking around the group. She dropped her eyes, at last, on the youngest two.

"Love them!" Max and Charles said together.

"Mary, I think their mother weaned them on oysters. You've met their grandparents, I suppose? They've introduced me to a variety of foods I never knew could be eaten," Fred laughed.

"Dear, gentle, Fred. A poet for a wife, three boys of various ages, a new baby, many different kinds of foods . . . It all has come upon you as quite a sudden plunge! Instead of old-fashioned comfort foods, you've had to learn to eat things from the sea and off the land." Mary gave Fred a pat on the back. "Well, good for you. I imagine, if being a father begins to age you, eating fresh produce will add years back to your life expectancy . . . The two forces coming together will even things out quite nicely."

During this time of introduction and greetings, the group stood beside the "Please Wait to be Seated " sign. Mary looked around for the restaurant host. "Now, where is my friend, the 'host of the day'? Ah there you are, Matthew. Not hiding, I hope. I come bringing a big crowd of hungry people with me. I called ahead for a table by the water."

"Yes, of course," said a thin little man with wire-rim glasses and balding head. "We have your favorite table ready, Miss Mary. I see two young gentlemen with you. Will you require, ahem, menus for those under twelve?"

Fred looked at the Max and Charles. He decided immediately such an action probably would not be wise. "No, these young men have adult tastes."

"But perhaps an easy-to-read menu for our friend John," Charles whispered to Fred with a devil-like grin.

"If Jean needs help I'm sure someone will help him," Fred said.

"I'll help Jean. He's after all the guest at our humble abode," Gabe said.

Gabe was Mary's youngest son. He was older than Jean, married, and the father of two daughters: Gretchen and Maryanne, who were close in age to Max and Charles.

"Ah, now that all the terribly difficult arrangements have been made, let us sit and enjoy this feast. Eat hearty. I'm no cook. Dinner tonight will be some sort of horrible leftovers or maybe a wonderful surprise," Mary said.

Their table was only a few feet from a wall of windows. A few yards beyond, the Chester River's glistening waves lapped at the pier. The seating was: Mary and Beth, heads together chit-chatting; Gabe and Jean laughing; Fred and the boys watching the river and just relaxing after an event-filled morning.

Matthew returned and was given orders for oysters every way they could be fixed. When he had retreated back to the kitchen, Mary, sitting at the head of the table, gave a brief history lesson.

"Everyone has studied the Boston Tea Party. It seems Boston had the best press. But, you see, between 1773 and 1774, 'tea parties' were held in many places. And do you know what these said tea parties actually were?" Mary asked. Not expecting an answer, she continued: "They were confrontations to prevent shipments of East India tea from entering the Colonies."

"Ee early colony pee-ple, they didn't like tea?" Jean asked.

"I've read where colonists enjoyed their tea greatly. In fact, an estimated 1,200,000 pounds of tea was sipped yearly. But, you see, the protests weren't about tea, actually, they were about being taxed. The colonists in many different places were united in their strong resistance to being taxed. I bet a phrase from school history lessons may still be hiding in some closet brain cells: 'Taxation ...'"

". . . without representation is tyranny'," Beth, Fred, and Gabe said together.

"Exactly. British Parliament repealed most of their taxes, but they were still holding on to a tea tax. And in 1773 the Tea Act was passed to help the ailing British East India Company establish a monopoly on the sale of tea in the American colonies. But the colonists believed it was another scheme to interfere with their freedom. So, they organized. They got the word out and

decided not to buy any imported goods. As for the tea .
. . well, as you know, it was not boiled and sipped from
lovely china tea cups. Oh, it's a complicated story, and
I'm afraid I'm so hungry my mind's a bit like a raw
oyster right now . . . very soft and slushy. Ah, but here's
Matthew, maybe he can help."

Matthew had arrived with warm corn muffins, glasses
of water, and several little white china tea pots.

"Thank you, Matthew. And, dear Matthew, I was
trying to explain Chestertown Tea Party history and well
. . . Do you know where information fliers on it may be
found?" Mary asked.

"Oh, indeed I do, Miss Mary. We have them right
here. I'll bring a few over for you and your guests.
They're left over from Memorial Day and won't be used
in 1985, because, you know, date and time changes, etc.
BUT Tea Party information printed on them is the same
as it has been since 1774."

"Perfect," Mary said. "Matthew, you answer two of my
most important needs: food and historical information."
When Matthew had gone to get the fliers, Mary said, "I
told you he is wonderful. He's always ready to go beyond
helpfulness."

Mary was a tall woman. Like Beth she had white hair,
but it was clipped short. Her cheeks were rosy, her skin
was tan, she loved exercise and was strong. She'd rather
be outside no matter what the weather, and when sailing
arrived, she was out on the water. She didn't have an
Eastern Shore nor even a Southern accent. In fact, she
was from Philadelphia and spoke as she'd been taught in

school: to enunciate every word, speak boldly and clearly, but to first and foremost, be a good listener. She was a poet, essay writer and playwright and had, on occasion, taught writing to children. But she preferred children outside of classrooms. She believed children should not be "hemmed in" by walls. "I do so hate walls, don't you?" she'd once asked Fred.

Matthew returned with a handful of fliers. He gave them to Mary. "Appetizers will be arriving soon," he said and was gone.

"Quickly! Matthew is always true to his word. If he says soon he means in minutes. We must look before our food arrives . . . what would you say, Jean? *Vite! Vite!*"

"*Oui*, Mary," Jean said.

"OK, here. Ah, yes, look on the back," said Mary. "Here's the most important information: a list of places and dates of tea parties back in the day." She read off the list for them:

"*Boston Tea Party: December 14, 1773.*"

"That's the one we study about in school," said Max.

"*December 22, 1773 in Charleston.* They didn't dump any tea but stored it instead, safe and locked away."

"*December 25, 1773 in Philadelphia.* Merry Christmas came but no tea, instead the ship went bye-bye without any delivery."

"*April 18, 1774 in New York City.* Spring had sprung and though tea was offered, it was never unloaded."

"*January 1774 in New Jersey.* Princeton College students made a wonderful bonfire to celebrate winter, using tea they took from where it had been hidden."

"Ahhhh! At last, here we are!" Mary exclaimed.

"Chestertown, Maryland: May 23, 1774. And yes, my dears, here, right outside this restaurant, the tea was dumped and a grand party was celebrated."

"Then . . ."

"October 14, 1774 in Annapolis. A ship and her cargo of tea all went up in smoke."

"September 23, 1774 in York, Maine. All sorts of things happened there, including some tea taken from off a ship, hidden, and perhaps enjoyed when the short days of cold began."

"December 22, 1774 , in Greenwich, New Jersey. Hidden tea was found, dumped in a field, and Colonial locals enjoyed a wonderful bonfire."

"Wow," said Max, "do I have lots to share when I get back in school! And to think two tea parties in Maryland, two in New Jersey, and a tea party even in Maine! All we've heard about is the one in Boston."

"All those little tea bags floating on the water," Charles murmured thoughtfully.

"The tea was loose back then, Charles. Geez," said Max. "Thank you, Mary, for all this information."

"You're very welcome, Max. Don't forget to thank Matthew. Oh, here he comes now with appetizers, raw oysters on the half shell. We'll toast our Chestertown Tea Party ancestors for dumping chests of tea here in the Chester River. First fix them as you like: cocktail sauce, lemon squeeze, or straight, then hold it up."

Matthew was thanked by all at the table, then oysters on the half shell were raised for a hearty toast by those sitting near Mary. One or two (who shall remain unnamed) picked up glasses of ice tea instead of juicy oysters.

"To the Chestertown Tea Party. Here! Here!" Mary proclaimed.

"Here! Here!" all repeated.

"Down the hatch!" Mary commanded.

At this instruction, seasoned raw oyster eaters placed gray, rough shells to their lips, tilted back their heads, and into their open mouths slurped down oysters.

Max thought of a poem he liked, written long ago by Lewis Carroll. In it a walrus and a carpenter take a walk on a beach where they convince young oysters to leave their comfy beds. *'A tragic poem. Poor oysters,'* Max thought. In his mind he heard the words of the last verse:

> *"O Oysters,' said the Carpenter,*
> *'You've had a pleasant run!*
> *Shall we be trotting home again?'*
> *But answer came there none —*
> *And this is scarcely odd, because*
> *They'd eaten every one."*

'I guess I'm being silly' Max thought. He bit into a crispy fried oyster that looked like a curly French fry. *'Not bad,'* he said to himself and ate another.

It was a glorious meal, oysters prepared all ways possible, but also other Eastern Shore favorites: fried chicken, pot pies, and fishy stews.

It was a meal filled with lots of conversations and storytelling.

Jean told stories about people and animals living in the little French towns he'd visited.

Beth described her summer theatre camps, the plays produced, and how her actors, ages eight to eighteen, packed up their sets and traveled around the countryside, setting up and performing in many places with audiences of all ages.

Mary said how grateful she was to the many who donated their time and talents to support Church Hill Theatre near Centreville. She described how a group of people had saved it just last year from being bulldozed for a parking lot. "Now this 1930s movie house will open again, showing films and hosting concerts and live theater."

After pies and apple brown betty for dessert, with filled tummies, the group said goodbye to Matthew.

"Now where to and what?" Charles asked Fred.

"Now we drive Miss Starry Eyes to finally meet other geese, including a special goose named Mr. Stubby," Fred told them.

Chapter 11

The Time of Goose 'Tails' Begins

"How far to Mary's house and goose freedom for Miss Starry Eyes?" Charles asked.

"From Chestertown, we travel sixteen miles on Route 213, then five more on a little road called Spaniard Neck. We make a final right. Mary's driveway is two miles long," Fred said to the travel-weary boys.

"Twenty-three miles," Charles said. "Bor-ing (sigh). Wake me when we get there." He nestled his head into an extra sweater he'd bunched into a pillow atop the armrest. He closed his eyes.

Charles had not slept well the night before. He didn't tell anybody, but wild-goose nightmares kept him from downy, sweet dreams. Instead of a peaceful sleep, he woke several times in the night, then back to sleep, and each time he had the same dream. It happened three times. *Three times.* In the dream it was late fall and he was in a field, surrounded by wild Canada geese grazing on corn. All was fine, then the geese all looked up at once, saw him, and with necks extended, heads nodding back and forth, giving warning "krrrr honk" calls, they'd headed right for Charles. Being surrounded by an entire flock of twenty-to-thirty pound geese, all with their necks extended, coming towards you, was not a funny sight. Nor a fun dream.

"Take a nap, Charles," said Max. "I'll wake you if we see something exciting, I promise. No fingers crossed behind my back."

"Ah, thanks," Charles said. He was already nodding off.

Fred turned the Hot Hits radio station down low and he and Max listened to Van Halen's "Jump," "I Just Called to Say I Love You" by Stevie Wonder, "Time After Time" by Cyndi Lauper, then Michael Jackson's "Thriller" and, just as they pulled off a narrow road onto Private Drive, "Ghostbusters" started playing again. Fred turned off the radio and put the truck into a lower gear, one best for slow driving. While Charles continued to sleep, Fred and Max stared out the windows.

On both sides of the narrow drive, gnarled old trees stood . . .

'They look like two groups of soldiers standing face to face. Brits versus Colonist? Yankees versus Confederates?' Max's imagination and all the history he'd heard that day blended as the truck crawled along.

Battered tree trunks were scarred by lightning strikes or years of gardeners pruning them back.

Max thought, *'I see hidden eyes. Each tree looks as if it's stretching . . . as if it's trying to stand as tall as its roots will let it.'*

"Look overhead," Fred whispered.

Looking, Max saw how tree branches formed a ceiling for this tree-tunnel lane. Twigs at the end of each branch looked like withered fingers, interlocked and clenched together.

At this moment Charles awakened. He sat up, mouth open. *This couldn't be only a driveway, could it?* Like Max and Fred, he dared not say anything aloud.

'Alice fell down through the rabbit's hole; we're not falling down, but like Alice we're entering a place like no other,' Max thought.

At the end of the long tunnel, the driveway turned into a path with farm fields on both sides. Fred continued driving slowly as chickens and ducks wandered from field to lane, crossing back and forth or ambling in front of the truck. A minute, two minutes, three minutes went by, then something of interest caught hen and duck eyes and they moved off the driveway, and Fred was finally able to pass these feathered speed fluffs.

Further down the drive the fields turned into a peach orchard: rows and rows of carefully pruned fruit trees stood beside new saplings, tied to stakes in preparation for their first winter. On the other side of the orchard there were groomed lawns and boxwood bushes. Then they arrived at an open space for vehicles to park under huge trees.

"Where's the house?" Max and Charles both asked.

"Look beyond that grove of trees," Fred pointed.

The boys stared, then saw the house.

It was three stories high, wood siding painted deep, dark green; window and door frames icy white. There was a little white picket fence, then a courtyard. They watched the back door open, then saw, and heard, Mary call:

"You made it! Congratulations. You've passed a test many fail. Come in, come in, your rooms await you, gentlemen. I'm sorry my husband isn't home to greet you. He was called to Baltimore on business. Isn't that interesting you all were crossing the Bay on the same day. Sadly, he'll not be home until next week. But someday, next time you visit, I hope you'll have a chance to meet him."

"Coming, Mary," Fred said. To the boys, "Grab your packs and other stuff, go find your room, then hurry back. We've neglected Miss Starry Eyes way too long."

"Yes sir," Max and Charles said.

They took their "stuff" from the cab, then, after Fred opened the back hatch, grabbed their backpacks and other bags.

They followed Mary's direction: "Up the stairs to the third floor, look for your room on the right. Be sure to look in the playroom on the left. There are some fine books, games, model sailing ships, other things. Bathroom down the back hall close to the bedroom. I'm sure you'll find it."

"Remember: find room, dump stuff, and hurry back," Fred called after the boys, who were racing to discover where they'd be sleeping.

"We have a goose to let loose," Fred said to Mary.

"Oh dear, that's right. The very patient goose, who hopefully will be charmed by our own Mr. Stubby. Come, Fred, I'll show you your room then let you get on with this very serious goose business. Afterwards, you must return and join Beth and me. We're settling our minds over scones and hot tea," Mary said.

"OK, this is a cool place to explore," Charles said, after giving a careful look at the bedroom with its old-fashioned, built-into-the-wall bunk beds, drawers built in under the bottom bed. There were many places where they could stash their things. Across the hall was a great sunny room: it might have once been called "the children's room."

" Let's hurry and get Miss Starry Eyes out of the truck and whatever else Fred thinks we must do, then come back to check these rooms," said Max.

"Yeah, yeah, right, but did you see this? Look at this model sailing ship. It must be a schooner. It has four masts and it's at full sail . . . very cool. And the view out this window! Geez, we're high up. We're in the treetops."

"I know, I know. Way cool, but we have goose business first," said Max. He was racing down the worn wooden steps. "Charles, check out these steps. It's like people have gone up and down them a million times. Look how worn they are in the middle."

"Old house. I bet Beth could tell tales about it."

Outside by the truck they found Fred waiting. Max and Charles scooted into the truck bed under the cap. A restless Miss Starry Eyes stared at them through the wire of her traveling cage.

"Slowly push her cage towards me," said Fred. "We'll leave her in it until Gabe tells us what time and where will be the best place for her to blend in. Mary called him at his house. He'll be here . . . Oh, I hear an engine now. It must be . . . Gabe," Fred said.

Max and Charles pushed the cage four feet into the waiting hands of Fred. Fred grabbed the cage with both hands, slowly lifted it and gently placed it on the grassy ground.

Max and Charles gathered some of Miss Starry Eyes favorite nibbles. By the time they'd jumped from the truck, Gabe had parked.

Every door of Gabe's vehicle opened. Out stepped Gabe and Jean, followed by Gabe's two young daughters. All were ready to meet Miss Starry Eyes.

'Gee, kids about our age' Max thought.

'Girls, well, there goes the fun' thought Charles.

"Max, Charles, meet Gretchen and Maryanne, ages ten and seven, in that order. Don't let their age fool you, they've been trained in the fine art of being 'Goose Gals'," said Gabe. "Gretchen and Maryanne, the taller guy is Max (he's eleven) and the other dude is Charles, eight going on forty-five. Just kidding, Charles."

Gabe looked at Miss Starry Eyes. "My, what a handsome Canada goose. How did you say you acquired her?"

"Our grandparents are animal rescue people. Certified and everything . . ." began Max.

"As we are here. Good. Good."

"Miss Starry Eyes was the only surviving gosling in

her clutch. It may have been a fox or weasel, but something got her parents and the others," Max told them. "A ranger on his daily rounds frightened off the murderer. He found Miss Starry Eyes alone amid the remains of shell chips, bones, and feathers. He kept her warm, wrapped in his jacket, and delivered her to Grandma and Grandpa's house. Both of our grandparents have taken care of hurt, sick, or abandoned animals. All kinds, but it was Grandma who raised Miss Starry Eyes."

"About how old is Miss Starry Eyes?" asked Gabe.

"She's three years old now. We have other geese at home. The big white ones . . ."

". . . Embden geese," inserted Fred.

"Yep," Max said. "But Miss Starry Eyes is our only Canada goose. She's been helping other goosey parents watch their babies, but now we think she needs to have . . . ah well . . ."

"She needs to find a Canada mate and have a life like other 'married' goose couples. She's three years old? Perfect age," Gabe said. "And it's early November, even better. Canada geese look for mates when they are about three years old, and they look in November. Your timing is excellent," Gabe said.

"We must take her down to the river . . ." Gretchen said.

"Yes, we must and now. I just saw Mr. Stubby grazing between the cornrows and the water right before we came," said Maryanne.

Max looked at Charles. These girls lived on a wildlife

preserve and they knew lots about nature. At least geese stuff.

"Go figure," muttered Charles to Max.

"The girls are right," said Gabe. "We'll take Miss Starry Eyes down where the corn has been harvested. The river bank is low there, making easy access to the water. Leave her dish and any food you've brought behind. It's time for her to sample our Centreville corn. I'll keep a good watch over her as she gets her bearings, eats, and drinks."

"We'll keep an eye on her too, Daddy," Gretchen said. "But can we show Max and Charles the corn maze you made for us and the old dock? We'll still be watching her . . . but from afar as she . . . gets adjusted."

"You go have fun. Fred and I'll keep an eye on her," Gabe said.

"I, too, have adventure," said Jean. "Maybe we play a drama game I know about refrigerators with milk in them on nights when the moon is full."

'Corn maze, river docks, and crazy drama games. Why not?' thought Max.

'At least we're not riding in the truck,' Charles thought.

"Good. Good," said Gabe.

Off they went across the lawn, headed to the fields: three men, two girls, and two boys with a goose in a wire cage. Miss Starry Eyes, who was all fluffed up, gave anyone who dared meet her gaze an evil eye. She'd come to the end of her goosey patience with all this carting-around business.

The girls ran ahead. Max, Charles, and Jean following

at a slower lope. Gabe and Fred, carrying Miss Starry Eyes, walked slowly, so as not to rock her cage more than necessary.

Around the side of the house, into the backyard. There, under a great oak tree, bundled in warm coats, resting on a bench, Mary and Beth sat holding mugs of something hot and talking nonstop.

Gretchen and Maryanne waved. "Helloooo, Gram. Helloooo, Beth. We'll be back in a while. We're giving the tour and helping settle Miss Starry Eyes," Gretchen called.

All waved to Mary and Beth.

"Cheers, my dears!" Mary said.

"Enjoy your adventures!" Beth called.

"Come on!" Maryanne yelled to Max and Charles, who were lagging behind. "We'll show you the big dock and then the maze!"

"How amazing," quipped Charles to Max.

But to Charles' surprise the dock was a great history lesson and the maze was really amazing after all.

In the past, the dock had been commercially used by local plantation owners. On specific days they'd bring crops of peaches, corn, and other farm-raised products. It was here, at this very dock, that large merchant ships arrived, tied up, unloaded things from Baltimore for local farmers and merchants living near Centreville. Then farmers' crops would be taken aboard. The exports from Centreville's locals went to Baltimore and, in some cases, other ports. In the beginning, sailing schooners were used, later on, steam-powered ships.

"But why your dock?" Charles asked. "What was so special about your dock?"

"Come on! We'll walk out on it. Maybe you'll understand better," Maryanne answered.

Max and Charles soon discovered what a long walk it was from beginning to the end of the pier. In the beginning they could look through clear, clean water to the sandy river bottom. They saw fish and even brown, helmet-like, prehistoric-looking horseshoe crabs in the water. Out further the water was deeper and deeper, the river's sandy bottom was further and further away, until they could no longer see it clearly through the wavy water.

When they reached the end, Gretchen said, "And this is why it was used . . . Our pier goes far out into the Chester River. Here the Chester is deep enough and wide enough for great ships to safely sail in and tie up."

"Do they still?" Charles asked.

"Oh, no, not now, but we still use it. Gram and Gramps have a sailboat. It's big enough to live on. They lived on it with Dad when he was our age. Gramps, Gram, and Dad sailed for two years. The Calvert School in Baltimore sent boxes of lesson plans and books needed for homeschooling for Dad. His classroom was the sailboat and Gram was his teacher. They still have the same sailboat. It's grand. We take trips sometimes on it with Dad, Mom, Gram, and Gramps. They teach us about waterways, coves, and marshes. We go on short sails and camp. It's fun. And we've crossed the Chesapeake Bay to Annapolis."

"You've sailed in a boat across the Chesapeake Bay? Was it scary?" Charles asked.

"Not really. Our family has all kinds of weather and navigation charts, modern gear. Plus, we never go when it's stormy," Maryanne said.

"Well," said Gretchen, "once when we sailed to the Western Shore, a storm came faster than we expected. Dad and Gramps had our ship well-anchored at the club in Annapolis, but it was still rolling and rocking so much Gram decided we should take a room at an inn. Which we did. It was great fun. We explored Annapolis and the Naval Academy. There was a football game at the Academy and they brought out their mascot. You know what it is, right?" Gretchen asked.

Charles looked at Max. Max thought a moment and then remembered all the funny stories he'd heard about games between West Point and Navy. He smiled. "Yep. A goat. You saw the Navy goat?"

"Yes, we did, and Navy won the game. We all loved the goat so much that when we were home again, we bothered Dad until he gave in. Now we have a few goats in our little barnyard. Maybe you'd like to see them later?" Gretchen asked.

"As long as they don't 'butt in'," Charles said.

All laughed.

"Good pun, Charles," Maryanne said.

"Can we see the sailboat, too?" Charles asked.

"Oh, no, sorry. She's put away for winter. Maybe, if you come another time . . . come spring, usually in May, she'll be out of dry dock. Maybe then Gramps or Dad will take us all for a day sail," Gretchen said.

"Yeah," said Max, "that would be fun."

"Yes," Charles agreed.

"*Oui*," said Jean, who had been standing nearby, letting the kids get acquainted.

"You sail, Jean?" Gretchen asked.

"Ah, *oui*, many times. Sailing is good way to boat . . . it make you think."

"You can't be lazy on the water when you are sailing. Sailing is work. You must tend the sails to catch the wind, and then, if all conditions are perfect, like a bird, you begin skimming on the waters. Good sailing calls for lots of skills," Gretchen said.

"You express like a poet, Gretchen," Jean said. "*Mais*, we must go. *Vite et* assist in goose happiness."

"Oh, yes. We must find Mr. Stubby. Earlier this morning he was here eating. Even this afternoon, I saw him, before we met you. He must have gone on a flight. He never goes far. He'll be returning soon," said Gretchen.

"Back to land, the Captain commands . . . all must walk the wooden plank of this ee pier!" Jean said dramatically. He waved one arm as if brandishing a sword.

"Jean, always the actor/drama coach," Maryanne said.

" '*All the world's a stage, and all the men and women merely players. They have their exits and their entrances . . .*' I think it is how Shakespeare wrote it, yes?" Jean said.

"Ah, Jean, good save," Gretchen laughed. "Yes, perfectly quoted. I just read the play with Gram and her play group. *As You Like It* is one of Shakespeare's comedies. OK, back to real time, everyone! Let's follow our commanding officer, Jean from France."

Walking faster back, watching the water become shallower, shallower, then soon they saw fish, crabs and the sandy river bottom.

"We reach shore once more! Who-rey!" Jean said.

"Sh!" Gretchen said. "Now, we must blend in with the wildlife and not scare the geese."

Quietly the five former "plank-walking pirates" went to join the landlubbers, Gabe and Fred, who were busy on their serious goose-watch mission. They were found near Miss Starry Eyes at the cornfield's edge, a few feet from the Chester's shore. No one wanted to disturb Miss Starry Eyes nor any wild Canada goose who might have come in early to feed and find rest for the night.

Miss Starry Eyes was out of her cage. She was stretching her wings, neck, legs, taking tiny steps, investigating her new surroundings. She found corn and without fear walked to the water's edge to scoop water into her bill and eat.

"Let's observe the action from back a few yards . . . here where the corn hasn't been cut. It'll be like our own 'goose blind'. Of course, we're not hunters, we're goose caretakers," Gabe whispered.

Into the rattling, dusty-dry world of old stalks and drooping, husk-covered ears of field corn, they went. Each picked their own observation place. Max and Charles stood next to each other. On Max's side, Gretchen stood. On her other side was Maryanne. Fred

In their goose blind, they could smell:

the mush odor of the yellow corn kernels;

damp-raw moist of crumbling earth;

nose-pinching, sneeze-seeking, raw green ragweed, after the early frost had turned its leaves, stalk and "berries" into black-green slime;

muddy marsh muck;

salty sweet of the Chester River waters.

Looking out, they observed Miss Starry Eyes as she contentedly nibbled and bill-dipped, stretched her neck, head high, and took drinks from the river. They heard her give "rrruffling" little purrs. She wasn't fearful. Instead she seemed at ease and curious.

"She's checking everything out. Good," said Gabe.

In a few moments, over their heads, they heard the sawing sound of wing feathers. Soon they saw a single goose flying slower and lower, with body rocking side to side, eyes wide.

"Look! Incoming goose!" Max said.

The goose made an awkward, feet-first landing, rippling calm river waters and creating a significant splash.

"That's our guy, Mr. Stubby. I'm afraid his landing skills are not impressive. I guess he didn't realize he was bring watched," Gabe said.

And watched he was. Miss Starry Eyes had heard and seen the entire display made by the gander pilot, but instead of ruffling feathers and fleeing the field, her reaction was to lift head, with bright eyes showing she was on high alert. Just who was this goose with feathers matching her own? Who was this goosey person who'd come to the shore she was enjoying? Was this his home spot or was he also a stranger? It didn't seem to enter her mind that she was the stranger visiting this goose's home turf.

"She say to him: 'Who are you? Why are you here visiting *my* new home?' Ee, a bit like what people might ask me," Jean whispered.

"I think that's exactly what she's thinking," Gabe said. "In the world of geese, the lady goose makes the important decisions."

"Really? Glad I'm not a goose," Charles said.

"Oh, what a goose I am," Maryanne whispered to Gretchen.

Max recognized the line. It was from a fairytale show he'd seen on video. He "hee-heed".

The girls looked at each other and giggled.

"Let's go back into the corn and give our two goose friends more space," Gabe said.

They regrouped another ten yards away . . . still close enough to watch, but not so close as to appear eavesdropping.

Gabe gathered them into a huddle and with the help of "goose-wise" daughters explained the wild ways of Canada geese.

"We humans have lots to learn from Canada geese," he began. "For one thing, they are loyal and faithful to each other. Once two geese bond in a 'wife-husband' type of partnership, they're true to each other until the end. If something happens to their partner, the other will remain single ever afterwards."

"They take their time. Actually, until they're three years old, right Dad? Before they decide who'll be their mate," said Gretchen.

"Exactly. While they're growing up, female geese stay and help other lady geese with their babies."

"Oh, we've seen Miss Starry Eyes do that," said Max. "She's helped 'gosling sit' for the white geese at our grandparents' house."

"Good. Good. Meanwhile, young ganders (boy geese) hang out with each other. Kind of like members of a young gentlemen's goose club. They're no longer allowed to be with their mom or dads; they're not yet the right age to find a mate. Finding a mate happens when they're three years old, too," Gabe explained.

"Since the female goose makes the decision, the guy goose has to win her heart by showing he's responsible and true. They . . . well, they date. While dating they talk a lot. Later, when they have babies, gander and goose are required to be responsible parents," Gretchen continued.

"Or else they lose the right to their babies. An older goose couple or a community of goose couples, called a 'creche', will take over and raise goslings, making sure they'll be safe," Maryanne said.

"They raise the babies and let the new couple go off, grow up, and learn to be better parents," Gabe said.

"Wow," said Max. "It's like in the human world when little kids are taken away and raised by others . . . sometimes by grandparents, sometimes in foster care."

"A lot like that. A community of geese raising goslings are wonderful, care-giving 'parents'."

"But I believe Miss Starry Eyes will be a great mom if she's ever given a chance," Max said.

"And we believe Mr. Stubby will be a great dad if he meets someone who doesn't mind his one leg is shorter than the other. He's so sweet and loving. Oh, listen, I can hear him talking goose talk to Miss Starry Eyes," Maryanne said.

"And I hear Miss Starry Eyes 'hrring' and murmuring back in her friendly way," said Charles.

As all watched and listened, the two young Canada geese conversed with each other. Heads up, heads down, necks were not stretched out, no bobbing heads, and no warning "honks."

Then Mr. Stubby, walking with his slight limp, headed back into the river with Miss Starry Eyes following three feet behind him.

"Oh my, this looks promising. Miss Starry Eyes is following Mr. Stubby. He's going to give her a little tour of the area. The water is calm. It's mid-afternoon. All is safe," said Gabe.

"First date. Eeh, so sweet, ey?" said Jean.

All agreed.

Chapter 12

Mazes and Games

"I'm going to stay here for a while and do my job as goose watcher. Fred, Mom, and Beth are waiting for you to join them for hot cocoa or tea."

"Dad, can we show Jean, Max, and Charles the corn maze?" Gretchen asked.

"Yes, of course. Now, guys, if you begin to feel lost in there, be sure to stop and give a signal," Gabe said.

"I know what we can use," said Max. "We have whistles. We even have codes? Right?" Max turned to Charles and Jean.

"Yep, have mine. Good idea, Max," Charles said. He took out the little whistle and gave two short notes.

"Great!" said Maryanne.

"This way to the entrance. I challenge you to find the exit," Gretchen said.

The girls took off with Jean, Max, and Charles following. They arrived at a wide break in the evenly spaced corn rows. A sign read: "Enter here . . . at your own risk."

"It should take about ten to fifteen minutes to get through the maze. If it takes longer blow your whistle. We'll come and save you."

"How will you know how to get out of the maze?" Charles asked Maryanne.

"Are you kidding? We designed it. We helped Dad cut it! We helped him build and decorate it. We've been using it ever since before Halloween," Maryanne said.

"It was a fundraiser for Gram's pet project: saving Church Hill Theatre. We charged people $3 ($1 for kids under twelve and free for babies). It was really a *fun* fundraiser. We made about $2,000, which we gave Gram. Was she ever surprised! And pleased," Gretchen told them.

"Two thousand dollars? Wee-hee, you are good at fun raising! *Bien!*" Jean exclaimed. "Okeey, I first go in. *Et* next one in count to . . . . ah, *vingt?*" If I don't appear in long time, come see if I lost or found." Jean entered the maze and soon disappeared. They could hear his sighs, "eeys" and occasional French exclamations.

"*Vingt* . . . twenty, right?" Max asked Gretchen.

"Yep. Count to twenty then follow Jean, but not too close. I don't think he's going in the right direction. We may have to save him," she said.

They all giggled. "Jean is twenty-three but sometimes acts like he's a little kid," Maryanne said, "We think it's because he's carefree and happy."

"Maybe because he's excited learning new things and places. He's only been in the U.S. a few days. Everything here is very new to him," said Max.

"Today Fred's been showing Jean and us things which are very OLD," Charles quipped.

"OK, Max, start counting. One . . . two," Gretchen said.

". . . three, four, five," Max counted, ". . . 17, 18, 19, 20!" He ran into the maze. Around the first bend, he found a little sign, bold, black-painted letters on an orange board: "Go right and find answers. Go left . . . you may reach the end."

'Fun. I think I'm like Lewis Carroll's character Alice when she had her adventures in Wonderland *and those backward reflections in* Looking Glass'

Max went right. He ran down another cut between towering dried cornstalks. At the end of this row, he discovered another bend, another choice, another sign: "When you make a U-Turn you . . . but when you see a black arrow on a white road sign, you go which way? Your choice."

'Well, if I make a U-turn, I go back to where I began. If I take a one-way arrow, I continue going forward' Max thought. He went straight.

The path through cornstalk rows became narrower and narrower until corn husks were brushing against both of Max's shoulders. Again, he thought of Alice. He thought of the times when she grew too big for places where she was. Up ahead he saw a place where bottoms of corn stalks were missing. Looking up, he saw the tops were tied together, making them look like the row was continuing on.

'Hmm, looks like an opening, a doorway without a door. I bet I'm to go through it,' Max thought. He went in. Inside he found a tunnel with stalks tied together about twelve inches over his head. The tunnel was about twelve feet long. Following it, he arrived at an open square of space, about ten feet by ten feet.

'Now, here's a puzzle,' Max thought. *'I see an opening on each side of this* room *with a sign to read at each doorway.'* Max read each sign:

This Way and you'll find . . . ears of corn waiting twelve months for another harvest time.
This Way you'll see bright stars on moonless nights and full moonbeams streaming a path over shimmering cold where ducks and geese paddle by.
This Way is only for the bold and fearless . . . or perhaps those who are thoughtless and reckless.
This Way rows rise up into little hills, places where chipmunks like to burrow. Those who love picking daisies in the grass will find chain necklace crowns glowing with yellow blooms.

'Oh, well, this time it's an easy choice,' thought Max, picking the open space by the last sign he had read about chipmunks and daisies. It was the right decision and soon Max was out of the maze. Once out, he found a table with a yellow daisy crown. It was his reward for picking the right way.

'Fun,' he thought.

"Hey, you made it!" Gretchen called. "You're the first one out. Maryanne went in last to see if she could rescue Jean and Charles. Shall we wait? Or go get some of Gram's hot cocoa?"

"Hot cocoa would taste great. You think ..." Just then Jean appeared. On his head he wore a cornhusk cap.

"I made it? Ah, *bien*! *Tres* funny, this maze. Good fun. See my hat? I made myself. Do you think it makes me look like a Colonist? I tried to make it have three corners, but corn wrappers are dry stuff and hard to make do what I want." He was laughing. He noticed Max's daisy crown. "Oh, Max look at you. I must bow. You must be the maze Daisy King wearing your crown."

Jean bowed. When he did, his husk hat fell to the ground. "Ah, pit-eee. Poor hat."

Just then they heard voices:

"I didn't need help!"

"Yes, you did. If you'd made that last turn, you'd have been in marsh mud up to your belly button!"

Charles and Maryanne emerged from the maze. Charles was red-faced and Maryanne had her arms crossed over her chest, carrying her head straight up. Her body language said it all, but so did her words: "No matter what you say, Charles, I'm the one who was right. You're the one who almost made a big mistake."

Jean clapped his hands together. All four young people turned their attention on him. He had assumed the role of teacher.

"All this emotion. Some good, hey? Some not good,

not good et all. So this what we do . . . we use it. We use emotions in a game. A game I tell you about before. So, here we go . . . this is what you must do. First, I team you up. Max your partner is. . . . Gretchen. And Charles, your partner is . . ."

"No way!"

"Hey, Charles, you not listening to me. I am tallest, so I'm in charge. Your partner in beginning will be . . . me. That makes Maryanne the boss. Maryanne, you will say words I tell you to say. And we must obey you. But then, halfway to house and hot cocoa rewards, I switch with you, and I be boss again. And then, Charles will be ready to play this game as it is to be played. So, here we go. These are the words you say. Max, you and me will say: 'The moon ee's beautiful tonight.' Gretchen and Charles, you must answer back, 'But there is no milk in the refrigerator'."

"Too easy," Charles said. He was not in a playing mood.

"Aw, Charles, Charles, what will I do with you, hey? This is the trick. You will be holding hands and running around, all over the lawn. And Maryanne calls out different emotions, then you must say your phrase using a new emotion."

"I don't understand," Charles said.

"Let me give exam," said Jean, taking Charles by the hands. "I say, like this: 'THE MOON IS BEAUTIFUL TONIGHT!!' and you say in same tone 'BUT THERE IS NO MILK IN THE REFRIGERATOR!!' Then Maryanne tell us a different emotion."

"Say it sadly," Maryanne said.

"Ah, good. So. Then I say, sadly, 'The moon, it is beautiful tonight, sniff'. And you, Charles, must say . . .'"

"'Sniff! but there's no milk in the refrigerator'," Charles said sadly. He was beginning to stop being angry.

"Good. Bien. But we hold hands, no matter what, we must keep a grip on each other hands and we must keep moving: we run in circles, we run slowly, we walk, we run again with our arms held high as we can get them to go. We run with our arms down as low, as low, as they go. And we must keep moving all over the lawn, but always heading towards the house. And when I say 'FREEZE', then we all stop. Then I be the Boss and take over calling out emotions and Maryanne takes hands with you, Charles, and the two of you play the same game, only this time, she get to say, 'But there is no milk in the refrigerator' . . . so, too, Gretchen and Max, you two switch, and say the phrase the other was saying. Any questions? No? Then we commence. Maryanne, begin us."

"Happy!" yelled Maryanne.

They ran up, down, slow, fast, in circles, in loops around each other, and as they moved, they said the two phrases: 'The moon is beautiful tonight' and 'But there is no milk in the refrigerator.'

Fifteen minutes later they were near the house, where Fred, Beth, and Mary were sitting on chairs and benches drinking hot tea and cocoa.

"Bravo!" Mary called. Beth and Fred clapped. The five winded players bowed, then collapsed on the grassy yard, panting.

"I think maybe something enriching would help them recover," Beth said. "What do you think, Mary?"

"I think it is time for mugs of cocoa with marshmallows. I even have peppermint sticks for stirring," Mary said. "Ah, look, see? Just the mention of cocoa and peppermint sticks have the little darh-lings stirring."

Indeed, all four children and Jean had gotten up from the soft lawn and were heading to the patio for homemade cookies and mugs of cocoa.

After refreshments, Jean and Fred went to see if Gabe needed help.

"And now, what will you four do, I wonder?" Mary asked Gretchen, Maryanne, Max, and Charles.

"Could we go to the playroom upstairs?" Charles asked.

"Oh, could we Gram? We could show the guys some of the wooden boats and books . . ." Maryanne said.

"And the board games are fun and the pickup sticks Gramps made for Dad when you were on that long sailing trip," Gretchen added.

"Oh, my. Hmmm," Mary said. She made a very serious face which in seconds melted into a smile. "But of course, darh-lings, I think that's most perfectly the right thing for you to do after all the outside play. You'll have more outside time later, so I've heard."

"Yeah!"

Max was last in line climbing up the stairs to the third-floor children's room. Maryanne was first. He watched her bobbing, long blond hair and thought it was as wild

as a lion's mane. Like Charles she was short, but unlike
Charles she was as quick and as wiry as a young goat.
Next up the stairs was Charles, Max thought, *'ambling'*,
a good word for his studious younger brother. Then
right in front of him was Gretchen, she with bobbed red
hair floating around her tanned face. She was dressed
like a boy might dress, then again, so was Maryanne.
Both girls looked as if they'd just come in from
mucking out horse stalls, crabbing, maybe sailing. But
though Gretchen might look like a farmer, she wore
some sweet scent, not daunting, not yucky like what
some girls his age wore in school and to after-school
sports. Gretchen wore the scent of spring flowers and
cool shady places.

"Max, are you coming?" Gretchen turned to face him.
She stood on the second floor landing.

"Yes." He began climbing the stairs, running one hand
along the dark, smooth, wooden rail.

"Dreaming up a scene from a play?" Gretchen called
down.

"Oh, no . . . well, maybe. Hadn't thought of it. I . . ."
He stumbled and then he knew what to say. "Just
thinking of a poem: 'halfway down the stairs' . . ."

"Oh, yes! Perfect you should mention it. A.A. Milne's
poem, 'Halfway Down,' from his book, *When We Were
Very Young*. But I don't think it's only for when we are
very young, do you, Max? I think it's everybody at any
age. Let's say it together."

And together they began reciting the poem. Each
knew every word.

By the time they'd reached the end of the poem, they were on the third floor.

"Great to know someone who likes 'children's' poems like that one," Max said.

"Actually, not so strange. Your mom's a poet and my grandmother is a poet and playwright."

They joined Charles and Maryanne, who were already examining all sizes, shapes, kinds of wooden toy ships, miniature row boats, and canoes. There was even a speedboat, a model that once had been used by traveling boat salesmen drumming up orders by showing off all the amenities these wooden beauties had.

After the grand tour of the children's room, the four broke into two pairs. Maryanne and Charles took boxes filled with all the makings for your own ship, found a table, two chairs, and began building a skipjack and a schooner. Gretchen and Max chose to work on several things. First a game of pick-up sticks using the set Gramps had made for Gabe. Next they emptied a big, round, cardboard tube filled with lots of real wooden logs, and each built a little log house. Finally, they settled in on a jigsaw puzzle of the Chester River.

Outside, the gray-white day was turning into sunset colors, and soon the early blackness of a November evening would begin.

Around 5 p.m. a van arrived. Fred got out and came in. He found the four still playing in the children's room.

"Maryanne, Gretchen, your dad is waiting in the van. You, your gram and Beth are to join him. We're all going to your house for a bonfire and hot dog roast. Jean is already there helping your mom get ready for the sudden invasion," Fred laughed.

"Ooo-kay!" Maryanne and Gretchen yipped. They both got up and ran to the doorway. Gretchen turned.

"Max, Charles, leave the room the way it is right now. We'll fix it straight tomorrow. Gram won't mind."

"Sure?" Fred asked.

"Yep. Gram always says, 'I can close the door.' See you soon! Wear warm clothes. Bring coats. The sea breeze off the river can get mean cold sometimes."

And they were gone.

"OK, you heard what Gretchen said: warm clothes and bring coats," Fred said.

"Hey, Fred, what are we to call Gabe's wife? Is she Gretchen and Maryanne's mom?" asked Max.

"Oh, sorry. Yes, she's their mom. Her name is Kat, short for Katherine, I guess. She loves cats. She's great. A naturalist, gardener, spins wool and knits. Dinner is said to be hot dogs, chips, and baked beans, but that's a modest description. The hot dogs are actually sausages from a local farmer, and Kat has been baking the beans, New England style, in a bean pot on a wood burning stove, all afternoon. The chips are homemade from potatoes they grew which they fry in olive oil. Gabe made a bonfire and Jean is tending it," Fred told them as they dressed in cords, wool socks, flannel shirts, sweaters, and wool-lined winter boots.

"What's the news on Miss Starry Eyes and Mr. Stubby?" Max asked.

"In one word? I'd say: 'Dating.' Gabe and I watched

them most of the afternoon. Mr. Stubby is quite the Eastern Shore gentleman. Miss Starry Eyes is a real lady. They've been talking, as you saw, from the start, goose talk and taking swims. Last I saw them they were both sitting near each other, looking at the sunset and 'krrrhonking' in soft murmurings like old friends."

"Romantic," Max said.

"Yuck," said Charles.

Chapter 13

Bonfire Dinner with Wynda Lutair, and Goose Down on a Full Moon

5:30 p.m. Everyone gathered at Gabe and Kat's house. Many years back it had been a barn on the farm. Gabe and some carpenter friends had turned it into a house while keeping much of the original "barnness." It had wide wooden floors, high ceilings with big beams, and much of it was open-space with walls only in areas like bedrooms and bathrooms. The yellow wood glowed from the low lamplight and burning candles. A few old trees sheltered the house from the hot Eastern Shore summer heat. It was close to the river but near the fields where wildlife gathered.

A picnic table and great tree logs for benches had been placed in a circle around a big steel fire ring. A bonfire crackled and snapped loudly. The river was near but the house protected them from most of the sea breezes.

Kat greeted Max and Charles like she had known them for a long time. She was friendly, easy, and just knew how to be with people of all ages. Like Maryanne, she had blond hair. Like Gretchen, her hair was cut short and tended to go every which way. She wore a man's tan canvas hunting coat with sleeves rolled up, and baggy corduroy pants hung over her work boots.

"The moon was full last night," Kat said. "It'll still be big and bright tonight. The clouds cleared away before sunset, the wind has died down. It's a good night for a bonfire dinner and maybe, after dinner, we can convince Beth to tell us a story?"

"I travel around and tell you things you should know about, if you know what I'm sayin'," Beth said, smiling.

"Wynda Lutair has returned," said Mary.

They roasted the sausage-dogs on long sticks, and each ate several helpings of the molasses-sweet baked beans and stacks of thick, homemade potato chips. Dessert was roast-your-own marshmallows on newly-cut sticks.

After dinner and cleanup, with the wood fire crackling, snapping, hissing, and putting out warm heat, it was time for Wynda Lutair to tell her tale:

Now, this be a long time ago an' in a world far from this one, but it was a world I knew well, you see? A world I was a wee one growing up in. Scott's Land it is called, you've heard of it? You know the place I'm talkin' 'bout?

Ah, but ye' don't know how it was back then. It was lovely. The air fresh and birds were singin' most every day. An' there lived a young man. His name was Richard. An' oh, Richard was a good lad, he was. A good lad an' he lived with his mom.

Sad to say his father had gone off an' he never returned. You know what I'm sayin? An' it made life hard for Richard an' his Mom workin' to keep the little farm they had an' pay the bills an' all an' they had no extra money. All the money they had went to pay bills. Except for a wee bit young Richard been savin', just in case he saw a chance to spend it on something important.

An' it got to be his Mom's birthday, an' you know, Richard, he bein' a good boy, he wanted to buy a present for his mom, not a big one, but he knew what she'd love, what she'd always had talked 'bout but never would she be spendin' money like that on herself. Still, Richard he knew his mom an' what she wanted most was an umbrella. An' so he was bound to get her one, don't you know, so when she'd go to church or, say, go to market, an' if the rains came, then she could put up an umbrella sweet as anything, an' not get all wet.

Richard, he had some coins he'd been given when he was born, an' some more he'd earned workin' side jobs, an' he got them out, then he took himself to market. There, don't you know, right away like, he saw a man with a half dozen fine gray, white, and black patterned umbrellas, one as handsome as the other. An' Richard decided, right there, he must have one for his mom.

But just as Richard was gettin' out his change purse an' 'bout to ask the merchant what he wanted for one of those fine umbrellas, dontcha you know, the merchant he began a puttin' those umbrellas away. He was closin' up. He was done his sellin' for one day.

Nobody was around. It were just Richard an' the man, but

*you know, I told you, Richard he was a good young man, an'
he didn't want to cause no trouble, so he watched the merchant
an' it was a strange thing he saw. Richard saw the merchant
pick up one umbrella at a time, an' each time he did, why . .
. the umbrella turned itself into a Canada goose, which the
merchant put in a sack.*

Richard could hardly believe his eyes.

*Each gray, black, white beautiful umbrella turned itself into
a big, fluffy, gray, black, white goose changin', dontcha know,
as it was a-goin' into that sack. Then when all umbrellas, now
geese, were in his sack-bag, the merchant put it into a cart he
had an' he headed back down a little path . . . he was headin'
back to his home, but you knew that.*

*Richard he decided he would follow the man with the cart
and big sack-bag full of geese/umbrellas. An' he did. An' it
was a long path, through what had been a cornfield, but now
it was near winter, so cornstalks were old, dried, an' rattlin' in
the wind like . . . well, like the sound of bones, you know
what I mean, cornstalks all rattlin' like skeletons, they were.*

*But Richard, dear lad, he never let it get to him. He knew
what he wanted an' it was a good want: he wanted a fine gift
for his mother.*

*Finally, with the full moon a pourin' down, making a path
of light, the old merchant arrived at his home and Richard not
far from him. Then, Richard he did see the merchant do the
strangest thing. Richard saw him open the sack-bag an', one
by one, take out a goose an' stick it on a roosting place an' all
Richard could see was fluffy feathers an' goose legs a hangin'
down . . . like the handles of umbrellas.*

After all of those geese was put to roost, the old merchant he went into his hut an' he closed the door. For a bit he had a lamp lit, but soon he must of blown it out an' gone to rest his own weary bones.

Now, Richard was a good boy, you know I said it before, but he really wanted a goose umbrella for his mom. So, he went over an' he looked up to where all those geese were on their roost and a sleep murmuring an' Richard he picked him out one, one he thought must be the prettiest, fluffiest, best goose umbrella he'd ever seen.

Then Richard . . . well, first he took out every coin he owned an' he placed those coins in a can he'd seen a sitting inside the cart. It was a can, that doncha know, had the symbol for money on it.

Do you know what I mean?

Good. I thought that you would.

Then, after Richard had given up all the money he had, he went back to the prettiest goose he'd ever seen an' he was gentle, as if he were a handlin' a newborn baby, an' he lifted that goose off of its roost an' he was about to start on his way back home when he noticed it wasn't any goose he was a carryin' but a giant toadstool.

Well, Richard was quite surprised an' put the toadstool down. Soon as that toadstool hit the ground, it flew up again to roost. It had turned itself back into a goose, pretty as you would please.

Richard went to another goose an' another until he'd tried to take all one by one an' in each case it was the same: each goose he took didn't turn into an umbrella but into a big, old toadstool.

Well, Richard, he was a sensitive young man, an' he was

feelin' frustrated an' sad at this point. He wasn't quite sure what he was goin' to do when he heard a noise. An' when he looked it was the merchant, but he didn't quite look the same as he had. The merchant was all rolled up in a feather down comforter to keep away the cold, don't-cha know, but as Richard was lookin' at him he noticed the merchant had a wattle under his chin an' my! weren't his legs naked, skinny an' scaly, more like turkey legs than a man's.

"An' what do you suppose you are doin' a followin' me home an' takin' my geese down one by one?" came a voice from the down comforter.

Now, Richard's mom had told him always tell the truth, an' so he did. He told it all an' he left nothin' out. He told how he wanted a fine umbrella for his mom. How he'd seen what the merchant had. How he'd planned to have bought one at the market, but the merchant had packed up. Richard told all he'd seen an' he told how he'd filled up the merchant man's can with all the coins he had because he had it in his mind to buy a goose/umbrella for his mom's birthday.

The merchant went, checked the can an' saw Richard was an honest young man. An' he said. "I'll pick out the goose for you an' you take it to your mother. But you must allow me to pick out the right goose."

"O, indeed, yes, of course," young Richard said.

"An' when you get this goose, you treat her sweet, you treat her kind. You listen to what she asks for an' you be sure to give her all she asks for. Then when your mother needs an umbrella, the prettiest of all umbrellas, she will be a wonderful umbrella just for your mom, nobody else. But back home, when she is not needed as an umbrella, she'll be a goose. An'

109

eventually, if you are kind, an' if your mother be kind to her, too, she will lay you lovely goose eggs. But they're not to be eaten. They are not to be hatched. They must be brought back to me. An' if you do all I say, an' if my goose is a happy goose an' if she lays eggs, an' if you, young sir, bring those eggs to me, I will make you one happy man, an' worries over money will never be yours again. Now, will you shake on this?"

An' you know they did.

Richard shook the hand and it felt more like a feathery wing than the muscle and skin of a person's hand.

An' a goose was given to Richard.

An', I tell you this is where the story could have one endin' or it could have another. It could be that all went well an' Richard, a good young man, honored the shake of a hand agreement, an' the goose was a good goose an' became an umbrella to keep off the rain, when Richard's mom needed an umbrella, an' during those in-between times the goose would lay eggs, an' Richard would take those eggs to the merchant. An' that, my young listeners, could be one endin' to the story.

But it is a bright full-moon night, like it was a bright, full-moon night a long, long time ago, in the place I be tellin' you about. An' on full-moon nights, things have enchantment an' become what they want to be . . . an' what harm can come to that?

Well, it remains to be seen, doesn't it? An' I am over this tale an' lettin' the endin' sit with you to be as you so wish it to be. An' you will see how it happens . . . you will see."

Wynda Lutair put her head down. She was done. She looked up and she was Beth again.

The audience sat in silence for a full two seconds, then all applauded, except Charles, who asked, "Could you tell us more? I'm not ready for the story to end."

But Max felt differently and said, "No, it pauses here . . . it ends and each of us has a chance to make up our own ending for it."

"Exactly," Beth said. "A living story doesn't end when the teller stops telling. A living story is born when a connection is made between the words and those who listen. The story grows bigger inside listeners, but this can only happen when the storyteller stops."

"I wish I could give Mom a goose umbrella," Max said. "Think of the fun she'd have every time she used it."

"I think your mother would find many poems hidden in goose umbrella feathers," Mary said. She turned to Beth, "Is this story a new one?"

"Ah, that you must be ask Wynda Lutair . . . but I think perhaps she may have thought of it visiting here and seeing again some Canada geese."

After saying thank you and good night to Kat, Gabe, and Jean, Mary caught a ride through the fields, back to her house, with Fred. Beth took Maryanne, Gretchen, Max, and Charles on the path through moonlit fields, near the corn maze, close to where Miss Starry Eyes and Mr. Stubby were last seen getting to know each other.

They followed the white glowing moon-path to Mary's house. The very long day now was night.

Nearby they heard murmuring sounds, many wings being preened, many sleepy sounds.

Charles clung close to Beth, "What's that noise? What are those shadows we see?" he asked. He thought of his scary goosey dreams.

"Shh, Charles, it's alright. It's only the sound hundreds of geese make having come here tonight, seeking a safe resting place. Come morning, ah, what a sound you may hear ... if you set your alarm clocks for dawn," Beth said.

Soon they reached the patio and then entered the house.

Mary greeted them. She told the girls to call their mom. She would come to get them in the van.

"Where's Dad?" asked Gretchen.

"Where's Fred?" Charles asked

"And Jean?" asked Maryanne.

"Oh, they've men's business to do," Beth said.

'Oh, wow, I bet I know,' Max thought, but he kept it to himself.

Soon, Kat arrived in the van and all said good night. Kat and the girls went home.

Mary told the boys, "See you in the morning. Don't forget to set your alarm clock for dawn. I wouldn't want you to sleep through the great rush of wings. Good night."

"Good dreams to you," Beth said.

"Goodnight," said Max.

"Night," Charles said, yawning.

Charles was soon snoring but Max was wide awake, wondering, 'Had Jean, Gabe, and Fred gone back to Chestertown to see if the ghost of Tallulah Bankhead might appear? Would she talk with visitors tonight?'

Chapter 14

Sunday, November 11, Sunrise Arrives, and We All Fly Away

Max had set the alarm for 6:25 a.m. Both boys woke and dressed immediately. By 6:30 they were looking out the window, through trees trunks, branches, twigs, ready for first beams of sunrise. Meanwhile, three stories below, and surrounding the house, they could hear murmurings, "krrhonks" and "errumhs."

"Max, did you look down? The field below us is filled with moving bodies," Charles said, pulling on his sweater. With one boot on, one carried in his hand, he ran to look out windows in the children's room. "And here, too! Every window I look through I see all these gray and white fluffy blobs moving. It looks like a feathery invasion! We're surrounded by . . ."

"Geese, Charles. Roosting geese, hurry. Pick a good window. I want to watch sunrise and see what might happen."

Just then they heard footsteps coming upstairs and then . . .

"All up and dressed?"

"Yes!" Max and Charles said together.

"Come on, young men. The best experience will be from the 'Widow's Walk'," said Beth. She entered the children's room and opened a door they'd not noticed before. "Quickly! This way!"

Max and Charles followed Beth up a narrow flight of stairs and through an open hatch. They found themselves in a 5-foot by 5-foot space with windows on every side, perched atop the old barn/house.

"Wow!"

"Awesome!"

"Cool!"

They looked through each window. Four stories below they saw geese in every field moving, ruffling feathers, stretching necks, with heads looking skyward. Hundreds of gray, black, and white bodies moving.

Together, Beth and the boys opened small side windows. The air was chilly but not freezing cold. With windows open they could better hear geese "talking."

Beth looked at a little watch she wore pinned to her sweater. "6:41."

With each second the morning sky colors became bolder and bolder: shades of maroon and gold. Looking through the east windows—"*Pop!*"—a glowing bright sun edge shed beams on the horizon.

At that same moment, as if all those below had been given a message heard only by wild geese and understood only by them, they began to take flight. The wing sounds and honking were almost deafening. The sound, sight, and wind produced by hundreds of geese rising from fields into the sky made the house feel as if it, too, would fly free, leaving its foundation behind. The house, with all inside, would fly away with the wild geese.

Beth, Max, and Charles were wide-eyed and speechless. What was happening was a beyond-description experience.

Afterwards. After every goose had flown away, such quiet filled the Widow's Walk and all of the house.

At last Beth spoke: "And now you know what you never knew before. Treasure it. You will carry it always in your memory. And, here's a thought, only an idea, maybe what just happened will change you for life," she sighed. "Breakfast will be at 8:00. It is 6:55. You could take a nap or . . . the choice is yours." She began descending the stairs.

Max and Charles watched until the sky was blue, first in the Widow's Walk, later back in their room. They didn't talk. For a while, Charles did nap on his bed. Max took out his notebooks and wrote: the time, the place, the date, and his guess at the number of geese.

Chapter 15

Breakfast Delights, Adults Sip Coffee and Tell Their Full-Moon Thriller Tale

7:55 a.m. Max and Charles descended the stairs. They followed the scent of fresh-brewed coffee to the dining room, where they found the table set and waiting. No one was there but a sleepy-looking Fred drinking a mug of coffee.

"Good morning?" Max asked.

"Hmm, maybe by my third mug, extra-strength," murmured Fred. "You guys sleep?"

"Oh, yeah. Great. We got up before sunrise and experienced the Goose Takeoff. Beth took us up into the Widow's Walk," said Charles.

"Yes. Pretty amazing, huh? I saw it down here . . . at ground level. Then I went back to bed."

"Long night?"

"One could say that." Fred took another drink of

coffee, put the mug down, rubbed his eyes with both hands. "But the story will wait until everyone's here." A few moments later they heard the noise of a vehicle pulling into the parking space beside the kitchen. Doors slammed. Then Jean, Gabe, Gretchen, and Maryanne came whooshing into the house, all carrying baskets and trays trailing wonderful baking smells.

"*Le petit dejeuner est arriver!*" said Jean, carrying a basket filled with tangerines and bananas. He was followed by a waltzing Gretchen with a tray of steaming sticky and cinnamon buns, with Maryanne next, creeping along as she carefully carried a covered dish filled with cooked bacon and sausages. Gabe was last with a giant crock. "Scrambled eggs!" he announced. "Kat sends the food, also her regrets. She can't be here. She's the Sunday School supervisor at the church we attend. She has to be there early to prepare for her teachers and students."

"What church? Is it St. Paul's Kent?" Fred asked.

"Oh, no. We go to Centreville United Methodist, also known as 'The Church on the Hill'," Gretchen said. "Mom said we could skip Sunday School today. We'll go to the 7 p.m. worship tonight. Night service is a mix of old stuff and new stuff with good music."

"We go to a Methodist church, too," said Max. "The minister is a friend of our mom's."

"Cool."

Mary and Beth joined the others at the big table. It could easily seat 12 people with plenty of elbow room.

'*A long, long table with many teapots, cups, saucers, plates and so much food! I hope this meal won't be like what Alice encountered with the Mad Hatter and the March Hare,'* Max thought.

"A feast! A feast!" Mary said. "Beth, I know you're a Sunday School teacher back home on the Western Shore. Could you grace our meal?"

"It would be my pleasure," Beth said. "Here's an old Scottish Blessing:

> *"Some hae meat and cannae eat,*
> *And some wad eat that want it;*
> *We hae meat, and we can eat,*
> *and sae the Lord to thankit."*

"And now let's eat and thankit to the ones who prepared and brought it!" Beth said.

When the meal was almost over except for second nibbles, fruit, and tiny peppermint candies, Mary looked at Fred, Jean, and Gabe. "So, where did you all disappear to last night after our wonderful bonfire dinner?"

Fred, Gabe, and Jean looked at each other.

"Okeeey," said Jean. "I gess it up to me to bee-gin. An' adventure we had . . . we will not forget, right, friends?"

"Unforgettable," Fred said.

"Agreed," said Gabe.

"We three brave men, after everybody go sleepy, geese and people, we drove to St. Paul's Kent Courtyard to visit grave of famous actress Tallulah Bankhead. Fred and Gabe said they'd read on some full-moon nights, people say they hear her talking."

Suddenly there was not a sound at the table. Everyone

stopped nibbling, sipping, some were holding their breaths.

"Driving over we discussed what we'd do if we found crowds of people there," Gabe said. "It is Veterans Day Weekend. There are tourists in town. We thought, certainly, some would be going to the cemetery and leaving presents on graves at midnight. Especially since it was only one night after the full moon."

"We decided if it was crowded we'd watch from afar, then leave after about fifteen minutes," said Fred.

"*Mais*, how you say . . . but?"

"Yes."

"But no, we drove to the graveyard *et* no *l'autos*. Not one. So, what we do? We must be brave. Go visit grave. We'd make pact to do so which we cannot break," Jean said.

"Lots of parking places. I parked and we got out. The moon shone on those white and gray granite gravestones, making them look like . . ."

"Like theatre lights, little lights on aisle floors, help you see your seat, only bigger," Jean added.

"The moon was bright. Almost light as day. We didn't need the flashlights we'd brought with us," Fred said.

"But we took them anyway," said Gabe.

"An' we go . . . we three brave men . . . we go down a worn path to Ms. Tallulah's grave."

"As we got closer we saw, indeed, piles of beads: yellow, green, and purple, Mardi Gras colors. And . . . we saw someone there . . ."

"Oh?"

"No?"

"My!"

"Goodness!"

"Yes, someone was there. Someone was sitting on the flat gravestone," said Fred.

"Typing on an old-fashioned Royal typewriter," added Gabe.

"A ver-ree pretty woman. She wearing a lady suit," Jean said.

"Oh, my lands," said Mary.

"A woman with a typewriter sitting on the gravestone? I've not heard of fairy folk described this way before," said Beth.

"Coooooool," Charles said, letting free a long-held breath.

"An' then I see even more. I see bottle of something on the stone beside her. A clear bottle with clear something, like water, in it. It had a red and silver label," Jean said.

"Vodka?" asked Mary.

"So it appeared," Gabe answered her.

"Then, she look up from typewriter. She stop typing. She place one hand on her brow *et* saluted us, Army style, then we all heard her . . . Right?" asked Jean, looking around at the other men.

"Yes."

"Indeed we did," said Gabe.

"She spoke to you?" Gretchen asked

"You actually heard her speaking?" asked Maryanne.

"Indeed? My lands! What did she say?" asked Mary.

"*How perfectly delicious for you to show up tonight, Dahlings!*" said Fred.

"*You've come for an interview with Connie Porter, how sweet,*" added Gabe.

"She laugh like this: *Hahahahah!*" imitated Jean.

"Then, as if dismissing us, she waved her hand and said . . ." Fred said.

"*. . . It's been divine!*" Fred, Jean and Gabe said altogether.

"But Connie Porter isn't the name carved on the gravestone," Maryanne said.

"No. It was the name of Tallulah Bankhead's famous character in her most famous movie," Gabe said.

"The movie was called *Life Boat* and Alfred Hitchcock directed it," Mary said.

The men nodded.

"Then what did you gentlemen do?" asked Beth.

"I'm afraid we weren't polite. We almost hurt each in our unruly 'let me out of here . . . get out of my way . . . you guys are on your own' scramble to run away as fast as we could run . . ." Gabe said.

". . . all of us galloped to the van. Thank heavens it has more than two doors. We all jumped in. For a moment we sat . . . breathing hard and saying, well, expressing our emotion," Fred said.

"Then I lookee back . . . back down the path we'd run up . . . an' in the distance, in the glowing moonlight distance . . . I see the woman, who been sitting. I see her stand an' look our way an' then I see her open her mouth and begin to laugh . . . at first I heard nothing.

Then, as if was following me, I heard her laugh closer an' closer like it chase after me. After us. An' it not the kind of laugh I ever want to join with."

"I heard it, too."

"So did I. That's when I turned the key in the ignition, put the van in gear, and we were out of there. I managed to stay inside the speed limit, but it was a battle. I wanted 'home' fast as I could get here," Gabe said.

"Tallulah Bankhead's spirit, you think?" Mary asked.

"I'm sure of it."

"It was that laugh. It was her laugh. I'd watched old television interviews and heard her laugh that way. I'd seen her on an episode of a *Lucy* show," Fred said.

"Whoa, pretty cool, Dad, Fred, Jean. When are you going to take Mom, Gretchen, and me to see this grave in the moonlight?" Maryanne said.

Max and Charles just stared at her. Was she kidding? Was she really that brave?

"Count me out," Gretchen said. "I'm sure Mom, too. As for Dad . . . I doubt he wants to make the trip anytime soon."

"No, sorry, sweetie. I need recovery time."

"Ees quite a story, *oui*?" Jean asked.

"Indeed it is," said Mary.

"I love the fact she appeared as the newspaper woman Connie Porter . . . if that was really Tallulah and not some actress impersonator," Beth said.

"I have a feeling it was no impersonator, but I'm not ever going back to look," Fred said.

"I hate to end this fine breakfast and all our thoughts

about last night, but I have to check on two geese who I hope are pairing up," said Gabe.

"Oh, do you think?" Max asked.

"Well, Max, the only way we'll know is by going down and watching," Gretchen said.

"Well, first, before the grand exodus, we must clean up our breakfast mess," Gabe said.

"No, you go ahead, Gabe," Fred said. "The boys and I will do the cleanup."

"Oh, Fred, thanks. OK, come on girls. Grab what we brought. We'll wash our bowls and trays down at the house. Thank you, Mom," he kissed Mary's cheek. "See you and Beth later today."

"After church. Yes. Thank you, Gabe, for bringing breakfast!" Mary said.

"Yes, thank you for this feast," said Beth.

Chapter 16

Goosey Goodbyes and Other Farewells

After cleanup Fred and the boys walked down through the fields to Gabe, Kat, and the girls' house. The sun beamed. The day was warmer than usual for November. There was a balmy light wind blowing sweet and salty air from the Chester River. It was quiet. The only sounds were of their footsteps, breathing and, when they were close to corn rows, a slight, crispy rattling from the dried husks.

"Peaceful here, hmm?" Fred asked.

"Sure is. It feels like we're far, far away from roads and towns, but actually we aren't far from Centreville and even the big city of Chestertown," Charles said.

"Like home, except at home we hear two roads near our house, the squeal of brakes, crazies racing in the middle of the night. And, instead of stars and the Milky

Way, we see the pink and white glow from Baltimore beaming across the sky," said Max.

"When your grandpa was growing up on The Property, it was like this. It's sad it has changed, but we're lucky, we still have woods to walk in, the springs, streams, and pond," Fred said.

"How fun it must be for Gretchen and Maryanne to have a river in their backyard and to live on a nature preserve," Max said with a sigh.

They arrived, near the river, where Gabe had introduced Miss Starry Eyes to Mr. Stubby. They looked around for Gabe and found him sitting on the ground near the "goose blind." He was dividing a large bag of corn into smaller bags. "Hey, over here," he said when he saw them.

They went over and sat beside him.

"I'm making small burlap bags of corn for Maryanne and Gretchen to carry over and spread around the fields, ones further away from the cornfield. And I'm keeping an eye out for our goosey couple."

"Any sign?" Max asked.

"Oh, yes. They've been coming and going. Right now, I think, they've gone exploring the river."

"Then things are going well?" Fred asked.

"Yes. I think these two have lots in common *and* they seem to be attracted to each other. A match, I'd say, but hang around. See for yourself."

"Want some help bagging corn?" Fred asked.

"I never turn down help," said Gabe. He handed them three small bags and they went to work filling them.

"Each should be about five pounds."

"Where's Jean and the girls?" Fred asked.

"Gone for a paddle in the row boat. They would have taken you but . . . not enough room. When they come back I'm sure, if you'd like, someone could take you out," Gabe said.

"Jean paddling?" asked Charles.

"Jean? Oh no, though I'm sure he could. No, Gretchen is the pro rower. She's taking classes in school so she can scull."

"Skull?" asked Charles. His imagination showed him a horrifying image.

"S-C-U-L-L , not S-K-U-L-L," said Gabe, laughing. "Around here it's one of the sports taught in our schools. Sculling boats are long and narrow. Many paddlers are needed. Team races are fierce. But Gretchen loves the sport and hopes one day to compete."

A *"krrhnk krrrrhonk"* sound came from the shore in front of them.

Gabe put his finger to his lips. Now was the time for watching and listening, not talking.

Webbed feet first, body turning side to side, one goose, followed by another, made awkward, wide-wake landings on the river. Side by side they paddled gracefully to shore. There was much goosey-type discussion when they were on the water, more when on the grassy lawn. The leader, Mr. Stubby, waited for the other goose. It was, indeed, Miss Starry Eyes. Side by side they walked beside the river. Heads up, sometimes held to one side, then once, twice, a third time, the two geese took turns touching bill to the other's neck or side.

"Love pecks," explained Gabe. "One of the ways a goose shows affection. You could say tiny kisses."

"Yuck!" said Charles.

"Ah, but Charles, they are two grown geese and you know . . ."

"I'm going to plug my ears," Charles said.

Fred looked at Gabe and winked. "I'm guessing it'll be OK to leave Miss Starry Eyes here? She's found the gander of her dreams?"

"Only the wild goose knows, but it looks like Mr. Stubby, too, has found the goose of his dreams. Yes, I think we have a match. Of course, I'll keep an eye on them. I know this farm is not what Miss Starry Eyes is used to, but Mr. Stubby has been on his own, with support from other ganders, for three years now. The greater community of geese, the creche, will keep an eye out on—close your ears, Charles—on the young couple," Gabe said.

"That was our goal . . . or one of the goals for this trip, right, Fred?" Max asked.

"Yep."

Goodbyes are hard when you must say goodbye to a pet you've watched grow, one you've fed and cared for. Goodbyes are hard between old friends, who you hope you'll see again. Goodbyes can be hard between new friends, special people, who you suddenly meet and who are fun to be with, people who teach you about who you are, who take you on adventures you may never have gone on had you not met them.

Saying goodbye to Miss Starry Eyes and Mr. Stubby was only the beginning of goodbyes that Sunday afternoon. Soon Fred, Max, and Charles were shaking hands goodbye with Gabe.

Next, funny guy Jean. "Hey, I see you soon. I have a job in Baltimore doing drama in schools with your mom. I hear I stay with you guys while I am doing the work. Hey, Fred, we look up some more ghosts? Hee-hee," laughed Jean.

Charles seemed to have no problem saying goodbye to Gretchen or with Maryanne. He did wish he'd had more chances to show Maryanne how he could outwit her at board games. But matching wits at games was something Charles did with the kids his age, and Maryanne was just another kid.

Max had trouble saying goodbye to Gretchen: "Hey, I hope you come up sometime. I can show you our little farm and Grandpa's trout hatchery," Max told her.

"Oh, cool! I hope you come down here again. I'm sorry I didn't get a chance to take you guys out rowing," Gretchen said.

At the house there was the goodbye to Mary and many *thank-yous* for all she'd done to make their visit special. "Darh-lings, I hope you come back again soon. I know you'll enjoy meeting my husband. A house with people in it is a home," Mary said.

Lastly, there was Beth, or Wynda Lutair.

"Oh, now, I'll be seeing you soon, you know? Your mom and I have a plan we'll put into action. Do you know what I'm saying? No, I can see you're looking a bit perplexed. Well, the Christmas season will be coming soon, and I've heard a play needs a few actors. I'll be in conversation with you . . . about being part of my Upper Nodd troupe. Do you think you'd like that? Be part of an acting troupe with other girls and boys in a play about Mr. Ebenezer Scrooge? Ah, now I've got you smiling. Good. Well, then. . . Good day to yah."

"Good day to yah!" Fred, Max, and Charles said as they each hugged Beth goodbye.

Then they were in the bright red truck. Soon the house and their friends were out of sight. Slowly, Fred drove down the tree-tunneled drive, away from the old farm with its many fields, away from the great river, and away from the world where many creatures were taken in and given safe refuge. No one spoke, but thoughts were busy as they each reflected on favorite moments spent during their Veterans Day Weekend on Maryland's Eastern Shore, November, 1984.

Epilogue

Places on the Fly Away Zone

The farm where Fred, Max, and Charles visited is a real place. Every year hundreds of Canada geese find safe refuge there. It is located on the Chester River, and the family farmers living there are wise to the ways of nature.

A few miles away there are shooting grounds where hunting duck and goose is allowed. Well-managed hunting fields, with guides assisting licensed hunters, is acceptable. But when creatures are wounded and suffer, or when hunters kill beyond set limits, then a delicate balance from "healthy" to "not healthy" is tipped and bad things begin to happen.

The history of Maryland's Eastern Shore is alive and well. Chestertown Tea Parties happen yearly, as do the celebrations on the courthouse steps in Centreville.

Washington College continues to invite writers to come, visit, lecture. The Church Hill Theatre is a tremendous success due to the support of artists and wonderful investors like Mary. Should you go to visit St. Paul's Kent Churchyard Cemetery, you'll still find what is thought to be the oldest swamp chestnut tree on Maryland's Eastern Shore. You'll also find the grave of Tallulah Bankhead, maybe decorated as it is described in this story.

Adventures are always waiting for us. As Wynda Lutair might have said:

"You know what I'm sayin'? Well, now, good day to ya' then."

The End

Suggestions for Further Reading

Canada Geese
http://www.preservewildlife.com/geeseworld.htm

Centreville, Maryland
The Church on the Hill — http://centreville-umc.com/
My Darling, Alice, Based on Letters and Legends of an Eastern Shore Farm 1837-1935 by Mary Wood (2002).

Chesapeake Bay Bridge
https://en.wikipedia.org/wiki/Chesapeake_Bay_Bridge

Chesapeake Ferries
"When Ferries Plied the Bay — Before bridges: For two centuries, Marylanders crossed shores by ship." *Sunday Sun Magazine* May 6, 2000, by Fred N. Rasmussen
http://articles.baltimoresun.com/2000-05-06/featur/0005060365_1_chesapeake-bay-bridge-ferry-boats-watermen

Chestertown, Maryland
St. Paul's Kent Episcopal Church — http://www.stpaulkent.org/
http://townofchestertown.com/visitors/for-history-buffs/

Chestertown Tea Party

The Star Democrat, Easton, MD, May 19, 2011
http://www.stardem.com/life/article_074a3d94-8442-
59ba-ade6-3e2e74947b75.html

Church Hill, Maryland

Church Hill Theatre —
http://www.churchhilltheatre.org/

Civil War

"Southern Sympathizers in Civil War Delmarva," by
Harold W. Hurst, *Tidewater Times*
http://tidewatertimes.com/HaroldW.Hurst-
October2006.htm

Currency Conversion

http://www.uwyo.edu/numimage/currency.htm

Storytelling

"Hearth Tales & Harp Strings" by Beth Vaughan and
Emily Reid. Music CD 2002.

Tallulah Bankhead

http://travelhag.com/2014/04/10/tallulah-bankhead-
grave-chestertown/
http://www.findagrave.com/php/famous.php?page=ce
m&FScemeteryid=640850
https://en.wikipedia.org/wiki/Tallulah_Bankhead

Tea Party General History
"Are There Instances of Raids Similar to the Boston Tea Party?" by John Buescher
National History Education Clearinghouse
http://teachinghistory.org/history-content/ask-a-historian/20657

Washington College and George Washington
https://www.washcoll.edu/about/college-history.php
https://en.wikipedia.org/wiki/George_Washington

CPSIA information can be obtained
at www.ICGtesting.com
Printed in the USA
FFOW03n0057110617
36501FF